AUTONOMOUS VILLAGE
The Dream Of A Social Entrepreneur

Vinod Ranaveni

FanatiXx Publication
ISO 9001:2015 CERTIFIED

FanatiXx Publication
AM/56, Basanti Colony, Rourkela 769012, Odisha
ISO 9001:2015 CERTIFIED
Website: *www.fanatixxpublication.com*

© Copyright, 2023, Vinod Ranaveni

All rights reserved. No part of this book may be reproduced, stored in a retrieval system, or transmitted, in any form by any means, electronic, mechanical, magnetic, optical, chemical, manual, photocopying, recording or otherwise, without prior written consent of the author.

"Autonomous Village- The Dream Of A Social Entrepreneur"
By: Vinod Ranaveni
ISBN: 978-93-5452-784-5
1st Edition
Cover Design: Sagar Samal
Price: 399.00 INR | $ 25
Printed and Typeset by: BooksClub.in

The opinions/ contents expressed in this book are solely of the author and do not represent the opinions/ stands/ thoughts of FanatiXx.

Disclaimer

This is a work of fiction. Names, characters, places, and incidents are either the product of author's imagination or have been used illustratively and any resemblance to any person, living or dead, events or locales is entirely coincidental.

Vinod Ranaveni asserts all rights to be identified as the author of this work.

About the Author

Vinod Ranaveni has been a "Co-Author" of 2 Anthologies 'LIFE IS BEAUTIFUL, BELIEVE IN IT' & 'DO IT FROM LOVE NOT FOR LOVE' and he started writing in 2016 for eternal happiness because when he writes, he is totally in a different world, and same happens when he plays a musical instrument. He also felt eternally happy when he helps someone or some species without any expectation.

He was born and raised in Rajaram, Telangana, and Lives in Mumbai, India. He Studied Master of Computer Applications (MCA) at SPIT College, Mumbai. He is Cloud Computing Enthusiastic with over 5+ years of strong IT experience in Public Clouds - Microsoft Azure, AWS, and GCP. His Hobbies are Writer, Playing an Instrument (Violin and Cajon), Watching Movies and Anime, Kung-Fu (Martial Arts & Tai-Chi), Drawing, and Social Service.

Acknowledgement

In my Life there are many things to acknowledge for writing this book and reaching so far in life.

I know it's lengthy but I wanted to specify every name who contributed to my life and book.

I would like to thank this beautiful life for giving me the opportunity to be alive and know more about life through its experiences of self and others in different phases to explore life to its fullest possibility. I am very grateful to contribute this legacy on behalf of me and my family to the nature and society so that it can help all those people in one or the other way who are reading it by giving their precious time and money into it.

This is not just a book, it's a beautiful journey of my life experiences where I spent my nights and days by analyzing and organizing it in such a way that readers can enjoy every part of the story by getting a different perspective of life so that they can explore and experience life in different ways.

I would like to thank my father, Bhumesh, for his contribution in my life. There are no words to express how grateful I am as his son and I am proud of saying, I am Bhumesh's Son. He contributed and dedicated his whole life to us to give us good standard of living in society in this competitive world. He has been my constant support, and now it's my turn to support him and accomplish his dream at any cost. My mother, Padma, his a homemaker where she spent all her life to make our home more beautiful. Her day starts and ends by thinking about us without taking care of her health and her life.

Both my Sisters, Vinitha and Vanitha supported me, took care of my health by making healthy and variety of food recipes whenever I am hungry. In some cases the new recipes would fail then at that time also they didn't worry because they know I am there to finish it no matter how taste it is. They both are very kind and take good care of me. Whenever I need help, both of them understand it before I tell them. Vanitha, I am very much inspired and learned by her dedication towards the work whenever she decides to do anything.

I want to thank both my Late Paternal and Maternal Grandparents for teaching me something about life through their living. Paternal Grandfather, Narsayya Ranaveni, taught me that people and respecting them are more important than money. Paternal Grandmother, Amrutha Ranaveni, is unable to hear and speak but still, she took good care of our family. She did all the other work that normal people did and she is brave to survive different villages. My maternal Grandfather, Acchabhoi Garige, He taught me one part of life should not mess whole life so always be ready to accept both the good and bad of every aspect of life and move on. My maternal Grandmother, DubbaRajam Garige, teaches me to give children fresh food and eat stale food for herself on his entire days. She took good care of her mother and father in their old age for years and she says, it is very important to do so to repay their debt to their parents. She gives respect to everyone in the village irrespective of their caste and helps anyone if needed. She used to give me her savings to buy toffee, fruits, and biscuits.

Dinesh Chiranjeevi Kodam: You taught me that one strong person in a family and his commitment towards life can change their entire family life.

Rajas Ramteke: Your calculations of money to manage a home with a little amount of money amazes me. Even though you received a gift of voice from nature, but still your efforts and dedication towards singing will give songs a new life.

Meena Tumma: Thanks for reading and encouraging me whenever I write any poems, stories, or comedy scripts.

Lavanya Messa: Your social media post about your achievement to become a compiler and co-author gave me different insights that I can also become an author and my official journey started to become a co-author and now become an author.

Swapnil Mhaske: I saw many people say, I want to become an entrepreneur and start it then they fail but you proved that anyone from a lower-level background can also become a successful entrepreneur by taking complete responsibility for the family on your shoulder since you are in a college.

Anuj Shivshankar Pandey: Your dedication, smart work, and hard work towards Kung Fu were so desperate that you sacrificed everything for it, decided and gave your 100% to learn it from the world wushu champion and professional coach.

Devendra Shivaji Karle: The way you make network connections and manage your family responsibilities with the balance of both profession and passion amazes me.

Late Laxmirajam Kashaiah Macha: I am very grateful to have you in my life as an inspiration where you shared your own experiences, solve my queries, and share stories to help me understand more about life. You are being punctual and dedicated your life to teaching even though it is a Government School. I didn't forget how kind you are to share tiffin with students who didn't bring food.

Shri Harshad Joshi: Thank you for supporting me without considering my age. Whenever I write anything about life or experiences, you listen to me very carefully, giving me advice and asking counter questions, helped me a lot to keep up with writings about life from a different perspective during our discussions. During our discussion, when I said that I want to write a book then you encouraged me to write a book and promised to help me during the process of writing book. That word gave me strength and I write the book.

Vikram Pariyar: Thank you for making me realize that 'Teaching is also an art which needs to be learned over a period of time by doing mistakes, recognizing them and recorrecting them, and also helping me when I am emotionally troubled during my young age.

Prabha: Thank you for giving me a specific direction when I am in trouble with having different knowledge of life and you gave me a specific person to reach out to so that I can blossom in life.

Dr. Pooja Raundale: To help students in every possible way using different platforms and you gave me one project which introduced me to music while working on it.

Dr. Aarti Milind Karande: To help students in every possible way by sharing workshop experience and knowledge with students and gave me direction towards my career by giving the advice to learn about Cloud.

Dr. Bharati Wukkadada: External visitor, she is open to listening to students' queries and their stories. I am very grateful to invite me to her home to spend some time and have dinner at her home. She is very kind and her food tastes well.

Dr. Santosh Gajanan Pathare: To learn multiple skills and connect with students through NSS. To teach students discipline and make students aware of different arts to give more options to students for their growth and development.

Mr. K Purushotham Reddy: He is the very joyful, kind, and cool person, I have ever seen. He is an expert in Teaching with unique styles as per students' interests.

Mrs. Nikhita Mangaonkar: By inviting an external speaker to tell us more about life where the demo was free but the workshop required money which students could not afford it. That day, I decided to write something about life and share it with everyone.

Mrs. Poonam Ameya Tare: To Give her 100% at teaching by explaining concepts and giving her own notes to students for easy remembering, and be friendly so that we can ask queries both in and out of topic.

Mrs. Divya B Shetty: Gave me the advice to do masters over job. Taking care of the entire IT department without any support and other resources. She published an IT book which gave me insights that anyone can publish if they have unique and valuable content.

Mr. Nistala Sarma: Expert in Teaching where he teaches and solves queries without seeing books and syllabus by giving practical and real-time examples.

I would like to thank everyone from Rajaram Village, Nearby Villages & Dharmapuri Municipality for providing me with more insights about different parts of life in different families. I would like to thank all those people who are responsible to represent and fulfilling their roles and responsibilities for the development and growth of village people, society, and nature. There are some people whom I want to thank you for their support and help for village growth, Bhimanna Soulla, Ashok Rangu, Bandari Murali, Naresh Soulla, other representatives and ward members of Rajaram as well as all representatives of the Municipal Body, other representatives and ward members of Dharmapuri.

I would like to thank my current and previous organizations with super supportive managers and colleagues for giving me advice whenever I was stuck during writing this book.

I would like to thank the entire "FanatiXx Publication" team to make this possible especially, the founder - Hemant Bansal for giving an opportunity to first time authors, the outreach manager- Ishika Bhardwaj for managing and coordinating throughout this process, the Editorial Manager - Saizal Gupta for your efforts and dedication towards editing the entire script word by word and proofreading whole script, again and again, to make it worth reading, Cover designer- Sagar Chand Samal, the greatest cover designer I could ever imagine.

Introduction

'Rajaram' is a small village in 'Telangana' (Dharmapuri, Jagtial) State, India, and is home to hundreds of families.

I am Sattayya, Sarpanch of the village, and I am married to two women named Pooja and Aarti. I married to the former because my father wanted me to make a family with Pooja. For the sake of my father's and Pooja's respect and reputation, I did not reject the proposal.
After a year, I confessed to my father and wife that I love someone else, who's in my college. I told them that I wanted to marry her back then, but since my values and heart were not ready to put Pooja's and my family's name at stake, I didn't utter a word. But when I came to know that the girl loves me too, and wanted to get hitched with me, despite knowing that I was already married, we both decided to tell you the truth and get married with your approval.

After listening to her husband speaking the truth, Pooja calmly said that she knows me well, she doesn't want me to live a double life; one with her, and the second with the other one. So, she agreed to mine and Aarti's marriage.
On the other hand, my father praised me for my honesty, & maturity. Currently, I am happily married to both, with three children. A boy, and a girl with Pooja, and a boy with Aarti.

There's a strange incident linked with my name being Vinod. When a child is born, he/she usually cries, but in my case it was the opposite. 'I didn't cry but smiled.' People who witnessed this were amazed and then on every face, there was joy and happiness, hence, my parents decided to name me 'Vinod'.

The name itself means doing something which makes others happy, apart from it other meanings are happiness, joy, pleasure, enjoyment, etc.

I finished my schooling and then went to college for further studies. My parents always supported me in concentrating on my studies.
One day my mother 'Aarti' said to me, "I need to talk to you."

"Yes, Mamma, tell me."

"This is the time where many adults start their journey of life with twists and turns. Some understand it and some don't. Some want to achieve something in life and some enjoy it. Most of the time, students get their guidance & queries solved by their friends who are unexperienced in life. I think they should get knowledge and experience from their teachers, parents, idols and experienced people to get to know every aspect of life and make decisions on their own wisely."

Let me share my experience of life so that it can help you in difficult times or in times of crucial decisions you need to make. My parents are very poor and they always worked hard to educate me. They always taught me to respect every individual irrespective of gender, caste, age, religion, status, etc. I asked them, "Why?" For that they said, "Every human being wants to be happy and wants to get respect from everyone. If you give respect to them then in turn, they will also give you respect. Most importantly help the needy people if you could without any expectations because help is help, it's not big or small. Some ask for it and most of them don't ask. At that time, you have to observe very carefully with your full attention to get to know their needs. The world is big, we know only a few people who are around us but most of them are strangers. Everyone is working for their family to fulfill their responsibility to get food, improve their standard of living, educate their children so that they can be independent and happy."

I used to eat in temples because they provided free food for those who are poor and poor people always pray & respect the food before eating.
During my college days, I understood the importance of food, money & power. I understood the value of people, love, happiness & compassion.

The important thing which I understood after observing 10 years of my life is, "Don't give money or food to anyone freely; instead of that teach them how to earn food or money by doing work, especially people who are capable of doing so that they can realize the value of it and learn new skills which can help them lifelong & make them independent."

Sacrificing Is Also Part of Love

This is how my mother shared all her experiences with me so that it can help me grow internally and externally to become mature enough to understand life, take decisions in difficult or crucial times and help others without any expectations.

My college was in the town of 'Jagtial'. During my college days, one day I went to a garden for a walk. I walked through the garden and sat on a chair in one corner. I saw a girl in another corner. She was giving biscuits to dogs, and seeds to birds. I saw that and felt good. I tried to see her but she was quite far. I could not see her face clearly. Next day, I went to the garden at the same time. First, I saw the same corner but was unable to find that girl. Later I saw all over the place but the garden was empty. I thought she had not come. I sat there on a bench, and after some time, I saw her coming & she sat next to my bench. She was very beautiful, especially her eyes and the smile on her face. When I saw her, I became speechless. I was shocked, my heart beat started to increase, there were no words to say anything, I felt like I had already met that person before. I saw my watch; it was time to go to college. I was in my 3rd year of graduation. While I was going home after college, there was a group of girls walking along the same path. I saw them and was shocked again. It was the same girl. I continued walking and heard someone calling my name from behind. It was the same girls' group; one of them was my old friend. She introduced me to that new girl mentioning her name, **"Sandhya"** and others. I introduced myself to that group. On the next day, I went to the garden and saw Sandhya. We became good friends & got to know each other over a period of 6 months.
One day I met her in the same garden and felt nervous.

Sandhya: Is everything alright? You seem a bit nervous. What happened?

Vinod: From the first day I saw you till date, I think a lot about you and it makes me feel very happy in a way that I can't express in words. Yesterday, I decided to express and share my feelings about you. I am in love with you and I want to be with you till my last breath."

Sandhya: I expected this from you, the way you are talking to me these days, but there is one thing I am hiding from you and that is, I am already in love with my school friend & our parents agreed with our relationship.

After listening to her, I was shattered. I felt like running away.

Sandhya: I am really sorry about this. If I knew, I would have told you before. Is it your first love?

Vinod: Yes.

Sandhya: I know it hurts but I am already in love & we are going to marry after completing our graduation. After spending so many days with you, I know you are a very good person. But if you really love me then right now you should concentrate on your career & take responsibility of your family because your parents are working so hard to educate you. During this process you will get another girl who will be a perfect match for you.

Vinod: I understand. And I am happy for you.

After 2 months, I went to the garden again at the same time. I did my walking & looked around. It was empty. After some time, suddenly Sandhya came near me and sat beside me.

Sandhya: How are you? Where have you been all these days? This being your first love, I was worried about you.

Vinod: I am good, I was not able to concentrate on anything in the 1st month. Later I managed to concentrate on my studies & my career. For the last 1 month, I was busy completing my syllabus for exams, so I didn't get time to come to the garden. Thank you for asking.

Sandhya: That's good, you are preparing in advance for exams which are after 3 months. I know, you want to know who I love. His name is "**Vikas**" & this is his photo. He is also in 3rd year in a different college.

I saw his photo; he was a very lucky person to have her with him. There was a change in my timetable so I was not able to go to the garden frequently anymore. One day, we both met and said goodbye to each other. After my exams, I went to the interview, and I saw all the candidates. I noticed one person who looked familiar. I realized it was Vikas, the same person whose photograph Sandhya showed me. After 3 rounds of interviews, we got to know there were 5 people selected for the HR Round but HR said they needed only 4 candidates. I saw the list; I had been selected. But I noticed Vikas' name was missing. I visited the cafeteria for some snacks and I found him sitting all alone. I approached him and we greeted each other.
I told him not to worry and he'll get another chance for sure.

Vikas: This is my 25th interview & this interviewer also did not select me. I don't know what is amiss and keeps me from being selected.

Vinod: Oh, 25th interview. Have you asked for feedback from HR?

Vikas: Yes, she said that I lack confidence and certifications too. After failing this many interviews my confidence is broken. As for these certifications, no one told me to do certifications during my college days.

Vinod: Don't worry, everything will be alright. Give some time to yourself.

HR: Hello Vikas, this is HR. You got selected.

Vikas: How?

HR: One of the selected candidates requested us to shortlist you instead of him. We were convinced by his explanation & selected you.

Vikas: Thank you so much ma'am.

Sandhya: After 2 years, I went to the garden to feed birds & dogs. When I went there and checked, food was already there. I asked the watchman about who had kept food here. He said that a man came daily in the morning & evening to give food. On the same day, I went in the evening to see who that person was. I saw the man and went near him. It was Vinod.

"Hi Vinod, how are you? It's been a long time & I'm shocked to see you here."

Vinod: Hi, I am good. I got to know about your marriage through my friends. How are you?

Sandhya: I am good. Is it you who comes daily and gives food to dogs and birds?

Vinod: Yes. I visit the garden daily and give food to both dogs and birds. I continued because I still love you. Doing activities of your interest makes me feel your presence.

Sandhya: I know you are a very kind person & my husband also came with me. Let me introduce you to him.

Vikas: Hey. I think I know him.
Sandhya: How?

Vikas: We both met during our interview process and he helped me gain confidence. He is the reason I got the job because after interview rounds were completed, I didn't get selected. Later I came to know that he convinced HR to replace him with me. I don't know why he did it. Can I ask you why you did that?

Vinod: I did that because I can easily crack another interview but for you it was difficult.

Vikas: Thank you for your help. By the way, what are you doing?

Vinod: I wanted to become a "Farmer", so that's what I am doing now. I am here in the town, learning about technology in order to be able to use it well for farming in my village because we have a farming business.

Later I bid them goodbye and while I was leaving, Sandhya gave me a smile.

'I know why you left the job,' thought Sandhya. We both smiled at each other and left.

This is my first love story which taught me to care for my love & respect my lover's interests.

Eat Food Prasad with Poor People & Always Think Of This Village As Your Family

While learning farming from my father, he taught me the importance of natural elements & fundamentals of life i.e., the Five Elements (Fire, Air, Space, Water & Earth). Seasons and climate have a lot to do with the location and other geological factors of a specific country. If you see, in India there are 3 natural seasons for different crops (Summer, Winter, and Monsoon). After having learned about technology in the town, I was now managing a farming business in my village,

After learning technology in town. I used to visit a temple in my village every day to eat food prasad with poor people. I used to donate everything that is required to make food for poor people in temples. It was my mother's wish that I do so, because, in her words **"we have more than what we need"**.

My brother was settled abroad, whereas I became the Sarpanch of my village as my father retired from the post. While taking over the post of Sarpanch from my father, he said, **"Always think of this village as your family**. This way you can understand what they need and what their problems are before they tell you."

One day, while I was eating food prasad with all devotees, I observed a new person. I observed him for a week & one day, I asked him about his details (his name, where he belonged to, and what he was doing here). Then the new person said, "Right now I can't tell you anything about me or any of my details." I respected him and resumed my daily work of farming and inspecting crop details.

I had some work in town as I was Sarpanch. I didn't always have time to eat prasad at the temple. So I visited the temple as and when I got time. After 1 month I again visited the temple to eat prasad and I noticed the new person was still there. After 2 days I revisited the temple but I didn't notice him. I asked all the people in the temple about him. One person said he had fallen ill a few days ago. I was worried about him and started searching the whole temple, enquiring about him from everyone I came across, but I didn't find any clue as to where he came from or where he stayed. Then I started searching nearby temples but I didn't find any information about him. It was almost night time but still I hadn't found him. I returned home and went to sleep. But I was unable to fall asleep. I got up, started my bike, and searched all over the village. Later in midnight I found a fire at the end of the village while driving on the road. I went there because I had never seen anything like that before. I went nearby and saw that the man I was looking for, lay on the ground, apparently sleeping. When I touched his body it was very hot, and it looked like he had a high fever. I tried to wake him up but he remained unconscious. I went to the doctor in my village and brought him here to examine the man. After examining he said, "Take him to the town hospital immediately." At night I took him to the town hospital and admitted him. I discussed with the Doctor and left. The doctor diagnosed him and provided necessary treatment. In the morning, when the man woke up, he asked the doctor who admitted me. The doctor said. "Vinod, your village Sarpanch." In the morning, when I went to the hospital to check on him, he had already left the hospital. I went to the place from where I had brought him to the hospital. I found him at that place and saw that he was fine. He was writing something. He saw me and thanked me for helping him at midnight. I said, "It's my pleasure, and you are a member of my family, so how could I not help you?" He said,"How is it that I am your family member? You don't even know my name." I said, "Family doesn't mean only blood relationships; Everybody who stays in this village is my family, so you are my family member." After listening to this he introduced himself, saying, "My name is **Dinesh** and I came here to spend some time by myself." Gradually, we both became good friends. We used to eat prasad at the temple & spend our spare time with each other. After a month, whenever I visited Dinesh at his place in the morning for a chat, I was not able to find him there. I visited his place a couple of times in the morning but still he was not there in the house. One day I met Dinesh at the temple in the evening and asked him where he would go in the morning.

The Journey of 11 Days

Dinesh: Before I tell you anything about it, I need 11 days of your time so that I can show you instead of telling.

There are 5 conditions you have to obey if you want to know.
1. You will not talk to anyone including me, but you can ask questions while observing if it's important.
2. I will explain things whenever required and you will listen to me carefully with full attention.
3. You have to observe what I say, and when the right time comes we will discuss these 11-days journey in detail.
4. I will take care of everything.
5. On the 12th day you are free to talk if you want.

Let me know when you are ready for it.

Vinod: Give me some time so that I can make arrangements for everything to work properly in my absence because I will need to be free from all my responsibilities for these 11-days journey. I need to inform my family about it as well, and take their permission for it.
After 3 days I met Dinesh and said that my family was initially worried but later I convinced them to allow this journey. They agreed to it.

We both started packing necessary things like food, medicines, clothes and money. After arranging for a vehicle, we started our journey for 11 days.
1st Day:
On the first day, we both checked into the hotel. We both freshened up, ate food and left for the day. We both visited the

Hospital. Dinesh talked to the hospital staff and they gave us hospital uniforms.

Dinesh: Listen, Vinod, we have to wear these uniforms and stand in the Delivery ward. Currently there are 5 deliveries scheduled. This is the starting point where Birth of human beings takes place. These human beings do not have any identity when they are born. Later their parents give identity to the newborn to identify in this world. Over here you have to observe both the mother and her child. The relationship between the mother and the child started 9 months back when the mother got pregnant. From being a single person to becoming a mother taking care of her child, mothers also undergo transformation right from the starting day of pregnancy as they form a special bond between mother and baby. During the delivery, the mother has to undergo tremendous pain to give birth to the child. After bearing that much pain, she also takes a new birth along with the baby. Mothers always focus on taking care of their newborn baby, but they ignore their own health. After delivery the doctor gives advice to couples saying the mother's physical health will change and she will get back pain, pelvic pain, stretching of muscles, incontinence, etc., in the future. When she gets old she might get some problems which are directly related to childbirth. If proper care is not taken for 1 to 2 years after childbirth, it can cause problems to the mother. It takes her a lot of time to regain her strength, and some physical therapies with proper care are required. As a husband you have to take care of the new mother and baby. When the baby becomes an adult, ask to take care of the mother. Once this is completed then we will go to the hotel.

Vinod: I have observed those 5 deliveries. After observing them, my respect towards all mothers has increased.

We then left from there. While returning to the hotel, Dinesh said, "Tomorrow morning, get up and freshen up, but don't eat anything.

2nd Day:
We both woke up and got ready. I didn't eat anything as Dinesh said, and I observed that he also didn't eat.

Dinesh: Today we are going to an **Orphanage**. Once we reach the Orphanage, wear the staff uniform that they will give and read the Register which contains every child's details. Go and check the entire Orphanage and observe each and every child very carefully from the time we reach there till we return to the hotel. This orphanage is very unique, as compared to other orphanages. I want you to observe and notice the difference. During lunch time you will distribute food to the children and later we will eat together. In the evening, we will leave for the day. In the Orphanage, some people come, having no choice but to survive on their own; some lose their parents, and some are brought here.

Vinod: Once we reached the Orphanage, I observed each and every child. We both distributed the food and ate later. I noticed the difference by observing the children, their rooms, classrooms, kitchen, bathrooms, garden area, sports area, library, etc. We both left for the day. During our journey back to the hotel, Dinesh said, "Tomorrow, you get up, eat food and be ready."

3rd Day:
Dinesh: Today we are going to a **Mental Hospital**. Once we reach there, wear the staff uniform that will be given. Go and check the entire Mental Hospital and observe each and every patient and staff member very carefully from the moment we reach till the time we return to the hotel. In the Mental Hospital, there are some patients who are taken care of by the hospital staff. There are certain patients who are taken care of by their family members. They come in the morning and leave in the evening.

There are some family members whose children were admitted here to be cured. Their family members joined here as staff to take care of other patients without any expectation. There are some other staff who were cured completely and they joined as a part of the staff. These patients are mentally challenged and very innocent, and they don't know about their minds as well as the external world. They all enjoy their own world here. But there are some people in the external world who are physically challenged but mentally healthy. They are just surviving and living without knowing that they have the power to change themselves & the world despite their physical disability. All they need is strong determination, along with some support and guidance, to change their destiny and that of others. There are some people in the external world who are physically and mentally healthy but have some small psychological problems because of which they suffer their whole life. In some cases, their family members, friends, neighbors also suffer. If they spend some time with themselves to observe and analyze the root cause of their suffering, then they can correct it to make their life beautiful.

Vinod: We have reached the Mental Hospital. I observed each and every patient and staff member very carefully. What Dinesh had said really made sense. I also observed the doctors who were treating the patients. We both left for the day. During our travel to the hotel, Dinesh said, "Tomorrow, get up, have food and be ready."

4th Day:
Dinesh: Today we are going to the **City**. In the City we are going to 4 places – 2 places in the morning and 2 places in the afternoon. We shall spend 3 hours at each place. You will observe each and every person with full attention. There are 2 types of postures you will use. First, you will sit in a chair and observe. Secondly, you'll stand and observe. In both postures you will be a statue such that no part of your body will move, and you will observe through your eyes. Your bare feet will touch the ground completely. From

Morning to Afternoon, you'll follow one posture, and from Afternoon to Evening, you will take the other posture. During the transit between 2 places, you will take rest.

Vinod: We reached the city and traveled to the most populated areas in the city. I observed each and every person with full attention. We both left from there. During our travel to the hotel, Dinesh said, "Tomorrow, get up and freshen up, but don't eat anything."

We both woke up and got ready. I didn't eat anything as Dinesh said, and I observed Dinesh also didn't eat.

5th Day:

Dinesh: Today we are going to **Prison**. Once we reach the Prison, wear their prisoner uniform that they will give and read the Register which contains every prisoner's criminal record, and the reason behind their crime. Go and check the entire Prison and observe each and every prisoner and staff member very carefully from the time we reach till we return to the hotel.

This Prison is very unique as compared to others. I want you to observe and notice the difference. During lunch time you will distribute food to the inmates and later we will eat together. In the evening, we will leave for the day. There are some prisoners who committed crimes genuinely because some wrong thing happened to them; some, for power or money because they see this is an easy way to achieve what they want; some did it accidentally or due to unstable emotions because of some incidents that happened in their life; some prisoners didn't do anything but the crime scene indicated them as the criminals and they didn't have any proofs or support to prove their innocence. As for the people who have a family or who did it accidentally or because of unstable emotions, if they love their family then they will accept the term and try to change themselves after release. The others will continue even when they are released. In prison, if they get an opportunity to live life happily by some counseling, support and guidance then they can change their life. But whether society will accept them or not totally makes a difference in their life. Society should accept them and their children because that person already got the punishment. The person who goes into jail and the person who comes out of jail are totally different persons.

Vinod: We have reached the prison. I observed each and every prisoner and staff member very carefully. What Dinesh was saying really made sense. I also observed the counselors who were guiding them. We both left for the day. During our travel to the hotel, Dinesh said, "Tomorrow, get up and freshen up, but don't eat anything.

We both woke up and got ready. I didn't eat anything, as Dinesh said, and I observed Dinesh also didn't eat.

6th Day:

Dinesh: Today we are going to an **Old Age Home**. Once we reach the Old Age Home, wear their staff uniform that they will give and read the register which contains every aged person's detail and the reason as to why they come here. Go and check the entire Old Age Home and observe each and every aged person very carefully from the time we reach till we return to the hotel.

This Old Age Home is very unique from other Old Age Homes. I want you to observe and notice the difference. During lunch time you will distribute food to them and later we will eat together. In the evening, we will leave for the day. The old people are like kids most of the time. Both the parents work for their family till retirement age to give their family a good standard of life. Only a few people do something for themselves to keep them going, and enjoy what they love to do. From the start of awareness of adulthood, if they spend some time with themselves and do what they love whenever they take some time for it then they will be zestful and keep others zestful around them. Parents understand

and love their children unconditionally but very few children who are now parents will love their parents and take care of them like kids. When the children are adults and married, they are unable to take care of and love their parents because of their own children. Once they are old and their children are, in turn, busy with their own children, then they realize how their parents must have felt. This is the cycle where very few people, when they are adults, take care of their children and their parents as kids, if they have the resources to give complete attention to their parents. Sometimes this is a good decision for old parents but parents have to understand and accept it.

Vinod: We have reached the Old Age Home.

I observed each and every senior citizen and staff member very carefully. What Dinesh said really made sense. I also observed, the old people were very happy, helping and supporting each other. We both left for the day. During our travel to the hotel, Dinesh said, "Tomorrow you get up , eat food and be ready."

7th Day:

Dinesh: Today we are going to the **Museum**. Once we reach the Museum, wear their staff uniform that they will give. This museum is an institution that houses a collection of artifacts and other objects of artistic, cultural, historical, or scientific importance. Read about every object which is present here and the reason why it is kept here. In this museum there is one section for "**Awards & Achievements**"; it indicates, "**Ordinary people can also do Extraordinary things if they are committed to put in effort and give time to it with patience, understanding and growth**". Every object that is kept here is the work of a person's entire life and contribution to the society, showcased, in his absence, as a memory. In the evening, we will leave for the day.

Vinod: We have reached the **Museum**. I observed each and every old object here and staff members very carefully. I also observed that the entire life of a person is encapsulated in the form of that object. We both left for the day. During our travel to the hotel, Dinesh said, "Tomorrow, you get up, eat food and be ready."

8th Day:
Dinesh: Today we are going to the **Library**. Once we reach the library, wear their staff uniform that they will give. A library is a collection of materials, books or media that are easily accessible for use. These collections help us to live a good standard of life and give us information in order to meet our needs on a daily basis. There are different categories which are available here and everything that is available here is shared on the basis of the information, perspective, knowledge and experience of multiple individuals to help future generations. In one category there are multiple things available because every person has their own perspective of seeing things and experiencing them. Every book or video that is put here is the work of a person's entire life and contribution to the society, preserved in memory of that person. In the evening, we will leave for the day.

Vinod: We have reached the library. I observed each and every category of books and media which will help us and our future generations. Every person has some need so they go through these categories and gain knowledge. We both left for the day. During our travel to the hotel, Dinesh said, "Tomorrow, get up and freshen up, but don't eat anything."

9th Day:
Dinesh: Today we are going to visit **Temples** of different religions. Once we reach those temples, go and check each and every temple, its pilgrims and staff members very carefully from the time we reach till we return to the hotel.

Every temple has some uniqueness. I want you to observe and notice the differences between each temple. During lunch time you will distribute food to the pilgrims and the priests, and later we both shall eat. In the evening, we will leave for the day. Every person comes to the temple to offer their prayers and love towards their respective God. Some people come to the temple to share their problems, to ask for forgiveness for the mistakes which they have committed knowingly or unknowingly, or to request God to fulfill their desires and support them. It is also important to take step-by-step actions towards their desires, goals, and ambitions, for which they need to have patience. Most of the people praying will restrict themselves to that particular god and the temple within the boundary wall. There are some unique people who extend the temple place to see the god in all living beings, and anonymously offer their help and support to serve those who are in need by donating food, money and their other requirements. In short, **Service to humans is service to God.** Whoever sees and experiences this wherever they are, always feels like they are in a temple.

Vinod: We have reached the Temples. I observed each and every temple, pilgrims, priests and other staff members. These temples play a vital role in giving strength to every individual in need of the support of God. We both left for the day. During our travel to the hotel, Dinesh said, "Tomorrow, get up and freshen up but don't eat anything."

10th Day:
Dinesh: Today we are going to visit different **Forests**. Once we reach these forests, go and check the beautiful natural scenery in and around the forest by sitting under the trees, near the rivers and on grass. **Feel the oneness with nature**. Take your food, keep it somewhere securely and observe. You see, there are other beings or species apart from human beings who live with us and consider this earth as their home. It is our responsibility to take care of Nature as much as possible, otherwise nature knows how to

balance itself. During lunch time we will keep some food around and observe it from a distance until it is finished. Later we both will eat. In the evening, we will leave for the day.

Vinod: We have visited different Forests. I observed each and every tree and its beauty. I spent some time in the company of nature and experienced the presence of other living. We both left for the day. During our travel to the hotel, Dinesh said, "Tomorrow, you get up and freshen up, but don't eat anything."

11th Day:

Dinesh: Today we are going to visit different **Graveyards** in the day time and at night, we will visit the **Post Mortem Ward**. Once we reach these Graveyards, go and see each site of burial. Till we return to the Post mortem ward, you must carefully observe the cemetery workers as well as the mourning family members, relatives and friends of the people who have died.

This is the reality of life which we call it "**Death**" where no one will escape from it and it is free of charge and priceless. It will come to everyone at one point in time wherever they are. It takes us away within a fraction of second and affects all our relations. Many people are afraid of it and do not accept it because of death's fear. They think they live forever here and live life accordingly. Only very few people are aware and ready to accept the reality of death, when they start experiencing life. They are the only ones who prepare for it and are ready to face it whenever it comes. They live life accordingly by helping and contributing to society in every possible way. It is evident that throughout their life, they spread love and happiness as much as possible. Only a few people close to them realize and experience love, compassion and happiness in their actions. They always take care and love the people around them when they are alive. When any dear one leaves them, they feel contented that they have given them their complete attention, love and care, being aware that everybody will leave one day, some early and some, late. But it is only when one's dear one leaves, that one will understand that one has taken care of that person and spent time with them while they were alive. Death shatters one's life completely till the point in time where one accepts it and moves on. Others will be unable to forgive themselves till they accept it. Some people worry and fear because they were completely dependent on someone, and now that person is gone. Hereafter, they have to depend on themselves in every aspect of life and give others their complete attention, love and care while they are alive. The most common ways of cremation are burning of the body on the funeral pyre, and burial of the body into soil.

Vinod: We have visited different Graveyards. I observed every burial site, every dead body being cremated, their relatives, friends and family members, and the graveyard workers very carefully. I spent some time observing and pondering on the reality of life. It made me silent from within.

We both left for the Post mortem ward of the hospital at night.

Dinesh: Once we reach the **Post Morten Ward**, wear their staff uniform that they will give. Go and see each and every dead body and the hospital staff very carefully. This is the first stage before "**Cremation**". Here the staff member will identify the dead body with its name and number tag. We will watch and experience the post mortem of a dead body. This is the reality of life. Only a few people can bear to see a dead body open. It requires a lot of strength to witness the corpse of a person. There are many things in life which are beyond imagination, and only very few people can experience it but they are unable to explain it to anyone about it or show it with proof. Later we will eat at night near dead bodies and sleep between dead bodies. In the morning we will leave for the hotel. From there we will reach the village and we will end our 11 days journey. Once we reach the village then you are free to talk and ask any questions if you have.

Vinod: We have reached the Post Morten Ward. I observed each and every dead body, the staff who are working here. We ate food in between dead bodies. I watched every dead body postmortem and at midnight we both slept between dead bodies. We both left in the morning to go to the village.

We both reached the village. Now I was free to talk and ask any questions but there was emptiness within me. I said bye to Dinesh and headed home.

When I visited my home, my mom asked me about the 11-days long journey. I told her that I visited the Hospital, Orphanage, Mental Hospital, City, Prison, Old Age Home, Museum, Library, Temples, Forests & Graveyard.

My mom said, "The person who planned this journey has seen life very closely. This is the journey that every person needs to take once in their life so that they can see every part of life. It will help them to discover life differently, and change the way they are currently living and their perspective of life".

On listening to this, my respect towards Dinesh increased. From the next day onwards, I was unable to concentrate on anything. There were many questions about life that arose in my mind, but I was unable to ask anyone. A week had passed since we both met. Finally, one day I visited Dinesh at his place and told him that I had many questions.

Dinesh: Before discussing your questions, I want to know what you have observed during our 11-days journey and now it's the right time to understand your observation level. I am able to understand your perspective of life, i.e., the extent to which you have observed everything. If you remember, this was my 3rd condition: "You have to observe what I say and when the right time arrives we will discuss this 11-days journey in detail". Now tell me everything that you have observed and experienced during our journey to the Hospital, Orphanage, Mental Hospital, City, Prison, Old Age Home, Museum, Library, Temples, Forests, Graveyards & Post Mortem Ward.

Vinod: Okay. Let's start with my **Observation** about the Hospital.

Hospital Observation:

When I stood in the Delivery Ward, I saw the pain that mothers went through to give birth to their baby. After giving birth to the baby when the baby cried, I saw the smile on the mother's face which is indescribable and can only be felt in one's heart. When the mother and the baby were shifted to the normal ward, the husband came to see the baby. First, he saw his wife, and both smiled. Then, the husband took the baby and held it in his arms for some time. The husband, on seeing his child, smiled and cried tears of joy. At the same time, he saw his wife and she also smiled. That was a very magical moment where both parents' hearts melted with love and felt the bond between husband, wife and child. In some cases, the husband kissed his wife and child on the forehead. I was left with an amazing feeling when I witnessed this occasion. The grandparents also were very happy. The mother has to take care of her child for 9 months, while both the parents have to take care of their child for the rest of their life. Over there, my respect towards all mothers and fathers increased. When I visited the doctor's room, I saw the happiness of the doctors and nurses. After every child birth, they also felt very happy that both mother and child were safe. In some cases, either the child or the mother or both lost their life due to some health complications during pregnancy. At that time, the husband, wife and their family went through tremendous pain which we can't even imagine. The doctors and nurses also cried and felt the pain. To give a good standard of living to their child, both parents sacrifice many things and that sacrifice seems very small when they see their child's happiness. I hope that when children grow up, they will understand all this and take care of their parents. Birth is a very beautiful occasion to see how life starts. The mother has to have patience for 9 months, taking care of herself every day, and then the baby is born. In the same way every human needs to perform their actions with patience in the right direction by seeing the reality of life.

Orphanage Observation:
When I went to the Orphanage, I went through the Register which contains every child's details explaining what they have gone

through before coming here. The reasons will melt our hearts and make us wonder how society can do this to innocent children for their benefits and desires. I saw why the children came to the orphanage and how they came here. The children take care of each other without asking anything; it's as if they know very well what others want by just caring for them, paying attention and observing other children. I saw the entire orphanage. It was very clean and they kept all the rooms, classrooms, kitchen, bathrooms, garden area, sports area, library very clean. They didn't wait for others to come and do chores or clean things. They did it by themselves. While eating food, they prayed for the farmers and the food first, then they ate. They didn't waste it or drop morsels of rice. They took only how much they could eat, in small quantities instead of taking it all at once. They distributed some food to the poor people who come to orphanages for meals, and some, to the birds, cats and dogs outside. In this way they understood and experienced happiness in helping and giving to needy people and animals. They love and respect everyone. All the children were very active and I observed that their behaviour was very stable and calm. It was as if their mind is calm instead of running with thoughts. I asked the staff there, how this was possible at such an age. They said, "They do the **'Stop & See' Exercise** which Dinesh taught all of us. All children sit or stand in a statue position and observe things and nature for hours or days. We explain things about life and once a child's mind is steady and calm then all the other children and their mind learn by observing and imitating. They are very clever in seeing the root cause of problems by doing brainstorming with all of us. They use technologies and devices very well." I was amazed on seeing this stability in them at such an early age.

Mental Hospital Observation:
When I went to the Mental Hospital, I saw the register to find out the patients' history and their details. When I saw all their medical history, I found some common reasons: Depression, genetics, stressful events like losing a loved one or being in a car or bike accident, brain chemistry, behavioral and emotional disorders in children, etc. I found some can be cured and some not. In many cases, mothers came to the hospital to take care of their children irrespective of their age. The doctors, nurses and staff were taking care of all the patients with love, compassion and affection. It didn't feel like they were doing their job; instead, it seemed like they were serving them with devotion and care. When I asked them about it, they said, "**By serving them we feel our life has meaning and it gives us happiness and peace within**".

City Observation:
When I went to the City, I remained like a statue in 2 postures. It was very difficult for me to hold the same posture for a long time but I had to do it. After an hour, I observed that there was stillness within me but outside, people were moving without stability. It was as if they were running in life without looking around. I could listen to my heartbeat, and feel my breath and the touch of air on my body. After I completed the task of staying motionless, I saw that there was stillness and calmness within me.

Prison Observation:
When I went to the Prison, I saw the register to find out prisoners' history and their details. When I saw all the prisoners' history to find out the reason for their imprisonment, I found that Dinesh was right. All prisoners fit in one category or the other. I could understand what their family must be going through in society. All the prisoners were happy and doing whatever task was assigned to them. When I saw a new prisoner who was coming, I

observed him as he was taken into the counseling room where the counselor said these things.

Counselor: I can understand, you did a crime knowingly or unknowingly but I want you to accept it. Till the end of your jail term here, live happily. If you have any hobbies then let us know we will arrange things for you but if you don't have any, please learn something new so that you can teach your children or others when you are out. If you do any work here, then we will send that money to your family. Take your time to understand things and settle here. If you have a life term then please think as if you are on a vacation or trip, and enjoy the rest of your life. You will become the guardian of this place.

I was very shocked to see the prison in such a way. When I observed other prisoners, they all were very happy and doing the tasks which were assigned to them. They help each other in the tasks and enjoyed themselves. Everyone here learnt cooking, gardening, interesting hobbies, etc. All jail bars don't have any locks. Every member in the jail is treated like a family member. They also respect food and consume it very judiciously, even giving food to animals, birds, fishes ,etc. I asked the counselor about this change in the prison:

Counselor: "**People are not used to living a happy and peaceful life**". All they know is **Fear and a Greedy Life** and they never sleep peacefully. We want to make the prison environment in such a way that "**People are used to living a happy and peaceful life**" so that they can realise that life can be lived happily and peacefully at any place; this way, they can sleep peacefully. Once they are habituated to this life then their life changes completely. In short, they shift their life from Violence to Peace.

Old Age Home Observation:

When I went to the Old Age Home, I saw the register containing every older person's details and reason why they came here.

When I saw all the old age people's history to find out the below reasons:
1. Children working away from home in another city, state or country.
2. Children lack in giving complete attention to their parents' needs, requirements, medical attention and care.
3. Misunderstanding between parents and children due to lack of communication.
4. They do not wish to be a burden to their kids and want to retire and spend their golden years independently.
5. Day and night medical attention.
6. Safety and Security.
7. Some are financially troubled.
8. Social interaction in a like-minded community.

I observed the reasons are valid for both sides and it's okay for old people to live in an Old age home as per their requirements. Here the old people were very happy, helping and supporting each other with the help of nursing staff. I saw them recording their "**Old Age Experiences and Advice**" for all, sharing what they had experienced over a period of time from different perspectives. There was one thought on the notice board of Old age home: "**By sharing your experience you can live forever on this earth**". It was like a treasure given by aged people to everyone.

Museum Observation:
When I went to the Museum, I saw a collection of artifacts and other objects of artistic, cultural, historical or scientific importance, displayed to the public. There were objects of beautiful forms, some man-made and some natural. There were some objects or artifacts which were the work of the lifetime of a person. They gave information about what the person had done in the past. There was some other information which was in the form of

diaries, documents, books, videos and other materials to refer to, whenever required.

Library Observation:
When I went to the Library, I saw that there were many collections in the form of books, quotes, documents, research papers, and audio and video media. I observed the passion, dedication, determination and consistency that people had put in for that work which might be successful or a failure. There are some people who, having observed their own work or that of others, feel a desire to share it with everyone to help mankind, so they document it in the form of books, documents, quotes, research papers, videos and audios. Now it is useful to us to keep evolving and to get a better standard of life by using these natural and man made resources. I owe my gratitude to everyone who gave their time and effort for it.

Temple Observation:
When I went to the Temples, I observed that every temple is unique. A temple is a beautiful place where people come alone or with their family to spend some time with themselves. Everyone comes to the temple for their own reasons. I saw a pilgrim with an attractive, bright and calm face and I felt that he was stable with his actions and peace within. But when I saw the others, who were coming, praying and going, I didn't feel that they really came here with devotion. Once they felt the devotion come from within them, they would automatically give love and care to everyone. It would be as if they extended their temple everywhere and served everyone in need without expecting anything, by seeing god in them. Devotion comes when you have gratitude towards everything you have, and respect everyone.

Forest Observation:

When I went to the Forests, I observed different kinds of trees and plants around the forest. Every tree was very unique in itself. I felt the calmness and stability of the trees when I stood beside a tree in statue position for an hour. Trees are amazing; every living being or species is dependent on them. They give all they have, even after they die, without expecting anything from other beings. Every species in the forest is so unique that they all have their lifespan living and death. Ant queens can live up to 30 years, and worker ants live from 1 to 3 years. All living beings who live in the forest are interdependent on one another. Every species has its own nature of living and uniqueness. The atmosphere and environment in a forest is very beautiful; it is full of life everywhere. Forests are in unity with nature and its elements (Fire, Air, Space, Water, & Earth). In the forest there is no one to talk to; one must only observe and experience life everywhere.

Graveyards Observation:
When I went to the Graveyards, I sat there. After some time, a dead body was brought by some people who were the deceased person's family, friends, neighbors and society. They all were saying different things about that person, some good and some bad. The family representative started the funeral rites and everybody watched him and touched his legs. They put wood on the body and started burning it. It just took 1 hour to completely burn the entire dead body. When I witnessed it, I saw that the person, now in the form of the dead body, didn't take anything with him. Nature took back all his body parts through its five elements. Everybody just stood and saw everything, but no one was accompanying the corpse in death. I went to different graveyards, but nobody departed with a dead body. Everybody has to die one day; the reason for death may be anything. I wondered why these people didn't think and accept, "**We have limited time so plan things accordingly, and utilize time and**

resources wisely to live and enjoy life". For some time in the graveyard, I saw and experienced the reality of life and emptiness within me. Someday, I would be here, burning, and there would be nothing I could take from here. I have decided to live each and every moment to the fullest so that there are no regrets in my final moments and I die happily, thanking nature for giving me the opportunity to live life here.

Post Mortem Ward Observation:

When I went to the Post Mortem Ward, I was shocked at first and there was some kind of fear within me when I looked at all the dead bodies around me. I saw that there was another dead body which came directly from a car accident. I saw the doctors were doing the post mortem of another body. While I was looking at the post mortem, I was completely blank, and could hear my own heartbeat. They were carefully removing all necessary internal organs. I saw the post mortem and this gave me a clear picture of the fact that everything that we collect over a period of time is gone. Everyone imagines and thinks about life in their mind in different ways and struggles for the rest of their life and now, this is the reality of life. Why don't they keep in mind, the reality that everything will be gone in just a fraction of a second? We think of reality in a different way but when our final moment arrives, we are shocked and unable to accept the reality at that moment and we are not in a position to tell anyone about this reality. It happens with everyone because everyone has to die no matter who they are.

I completely thank you, Dinesh, for giving me such insights about life at an early stage of my life so that I can live life by accepting the reality. When I was eating food in between When I stood next to the dead bodies, I felt gratitude for the life and food that I have. I held the hand of the dead body and thanked the dead body too. I slept peacefully that night, having accepted death.

This is all I have **observed** in all those places during our journey of 11 days.

Basic/Common Questions and Answers

Dinesh: Vinod, your observation and analyzing skills are amazing. There is one important thing that I want to tell you before discussing about your questions. The reason behind the 1st condition ("you will not talk to anyone including me") is that until and unless you see a complete picture of life from birth to death you will always have questions from different perspectives in different stages of life. Every question has an answer in 3 phases.
1. Your answer is based on your knowledge, observation, perspective and experience.
2. Others answer is based on their knowledge, observation, perspective and experience.
3. The real answer to the question is simple and clear but everybody makes it complex because of their knowledge, observation, perspective and experience.

We can't hold a question for a long time; all we want is answers to our questions no matter where we are getting those answers from, and we don't want to know whether they are true or not. "**Everybody wants to know everything.**" That's why if anyone asks them anything, they say "**I know this and this is how it is.**" Very few people genuinely say "**I don't know. Please ask others or look for other sources**". But once you get the real answer to a single basic question, then you understand "**How to find an answer to any question**". Here you don't need to prove anything to anyone. You can ask me, "How will you know whether your answer is real or not?" It's simple. **If your answer makes you calm then it's the real answer.** If not then you have to dig deep down and stay with the question for some more time. This is where observation with full attention and focus comes into the picture, to see the reality which is simple in most of the times. Let's begin with your questions.

Vinod: I got clarity about the questions and answers. These are some questions which are on my mind. As I have understood so far, **"the human beings who were born on this planet have to leave one day"** so what is life? Why do we live? Is there any purpose to us? Why are we born and why do we die? What is this world? What is body and mind? Then what is the difference between a body and a dead body? Why do people look unique and why are there differences in people if everyone has the same body and mind? What is the source of all energy? Who decides whether the child will be born into a rich family or a poor family or a middle-income family? What is karma? What is power? Why do people kill each other for power? Is everything already defined? What are emotions? Everyone has to leave empty-handed one day so why are these people working and collecting things (material and non-material)? What are these relations? What is the reality of this cycle of birth and death? What is love? What is happiness? What is compassion? Why to marry? What is the purpose of marriage? Why do different countries have different rules? Why do we do rituals after death? What is culture? Why do we have festivals? What is consciousness? What is awareness? Why do people die (some early or late or in the middle)? What exactly happens before birth and after death? Why are people suffering from all the things around us? What are rules, responsibility, roles, laws, government, society and environment? What is sex & what is the purpose of it? Why do we attract towards same or different gender irrespective of age? Where do all these scriptures come from? Where do all these stories come from? Are all these things around us real or imaginary? Where we are heading towards? Why do people live in fear of death each and every day? Why do people go into depression? Why are people suffering from addictions? What is the purpose of life, birth & death? What are these desires and emotions? What is good and bad? Who decides which person should live for how much time (on the basis of what factors)? Why do people hate and kill each other? Why do people commit suicide? Why do people have addictions? Why are people addicted to addictions? What is friendship? Is the ghost real? What is ego? What is spirituality? What is black magic? Is God real? What is sleep & why do we sleep? Why do we eat? Why do we think? Why do incidents and accidents happen in life? Does life teach anything to human beings? What is Nature? Does nature teach anything to human beings? What is this planet or earth? Why are we here on this planet or earth? There are many queries but this is all as of now.

Dinesh: All these queries will get addressed by yourself in time when you are in a position to understand the real answer. I don't think my answers will satisfy you. But there's one piece of advice I can give you, which helped me : **Find a place where no one disturbs you for some time and spend some time with yourself along with these questions**. Some questions can get answers in one second, while some questions take days, weeks, months or years. You have to be patient and sit with the questions till you get answers. I spend some time alone to observe and be aware of our unity with nature through the fundamentals of life i.e. the five elements (Fire, Air, Space, Water & Earth). Sit and close your eyes and think in depth about the day-to-day activities that you have done so far. Observe and Analyze people around you. Once you analyze that then you will learn and get an answer when it's the right time. Later that will help you to become mature to understand others and yourself by observing their actions and yours.

Some questions will get addressed and some won't, so don't worry. It's not as though you will get all answers to all questions at the same time. Some questions are created by the mind, and some, by people and the surroundings, so be calm and happy. You will get the answers when the right time comes and you are in a position to understand it. Once you understand and experience the existence of your life then everything will fall into place.

Vinod: Okay, I got it. Does All these things will be applicable to every individual person?

Dinesh: Yes, this is applicable to every individual person because our body looks different but the source of the body is the same for all.

Vinod: Thank you so much for your clarification. Now it makes me calm because all these questions were on my mind, due to which I was not able to focus and concentrate on anything.

Dinesh: It's been a long time since we talked. I would suggest you to go home and take a rest. We will resume this discussion tomorrow at the temple.

Vinod: It's fine. Let's meet tomorrow at the temple.

We both met at a temple. Later we went near the river in the village. We resumed our discussion.

Vinod: Dinesh, I want to ask you something if you are comfortable with it.

Dinesh: Yes, please ask.

Vinod: Who are you? Where do you come from? Why are you staying here? Don't you have a family?

Dinesh: I will tell you when the right time comes but now I want to ask you some questions.

Vinod: Yes, please.

Dinesh: How many people are there on this earth?

Vinod: Around 8 Billion and more in the future.

Dinesh: How many species are there including humans?
Vinod: There are many species, some identified with their name and type, but some are still unknown.

Dinesh: What is common in all of them?

Vinod: They all take birth, eat food, survive, sleep, reproduce, protect themselves & die.

Dinesh: What is the difference between human beings & other species?

Vinod: Mind, emotions, and the ability to use one's mind wisely to do things, think and observe, and for time recognition, analyzing of past, present, future, desires, and growth, and evolving of things around us.

Dinesh: Okay, as you said. Every human being has some common things like mind (ability to utilize it and think), time (to recognize past, present and future), emotions (happiness, sadness, fear, disgust, anger & surprise), desires (for self, family, society, country and world). But people are unique irrespective of all these common things. Do you know what makes them unique?

Vinod: Yes, as per my understanding, what they do, that is, their desires and actions.

Dinesh: Their respective desires and actions are what makes them unique but there are a lot of things that depend on this. Some common desires are: their growth in their respective family, society, culture, resources they have to live with and resources they want, standard of living and many more. Do you know What are the most important fundamental things? what everyone is looking for & why? and where does everyone want to reach out in any way?

Vinod: The most important fundamental things are food, health, respect, happiness, love, safety, security, sleep and surviving. People look for a good standard of living for themselves and their children. Everyone wants to get respect, recognition, acknowledgement, name, fame and money so that they can reach out higher level in the society.

Dinesh: You are right. Do you know why people struggle to live and are not satisfied with the things that they have and always looking for something that they don't have?

Vinod: I don't know.

Dinesh: They are not satisfied with what they have because they always live either in the past or future. If they are living in the past then they always think about it and are stuck there only either in pain of losing something or in the memory of something. If they live in the future they always want more & are not satisfied with what they have. Most of the times they are always looking for something or the other because they are not silent, stable and calm to see what they have. If they are able to stop and see things around them then they will utilize the existing things to achieve what they want in life with the things they have. To be silent, stable and calm, they have to stop themselves to experience the present moment because everything is available in the present moment. If people are able to live in the present moment then they realize & experience the importance of this beautiful life. Time is something which makes us see the differences of past, present and future. Space is something which stands between things and people and makes us think we are different from each other. There is one more common thing which is unique for all common beings is "**Natural Elements**". There are 5 natural elements i.e.**Fire, Air, Space, Water & Earth**. These natural elements are fundamentals of every individual species and there are some "**Natural Resources**" that help us to survive and live life. The time seems to pass because of these resources and along with these, the major resources are the sun & the moon. Along with these elements and resources, there are seasons that take place differently in different locations based on the weather all over the world. Once people recognise these fundamental things and accept them as they are, they start realizing the meaning of life. Once they start realizing the meaning of life, they start thinking about life. Then they ask the questions that you asked, which are common for everyone. Based on the life that they are currently living, some find answers to their questions and realize life, then they give meaning to their life with their desires, goals, ambitions, vision, mission and actions instead of waiting for the meaning to come into their life.

Vinod: I got to know some important fundamental elements of life. But how to live in the present moment? By knowing all these things or how?

Dinesh: To live the present moment, firstly, people need to understand the body because the body is the source of our existence on this planet. Otherwise how do we know that we exist?

To know more details about the body, we have to understand how the body works. What is it made up of? What are the different parts of the body? There are some important parts of the body which help us to survive and live life by using those body parts. The Human body is naturally made in such a way that it is capable of doing things by taking decisions, thinking, observing, analyzing and comparing. There are many things that are happening from the central part of the body i.e. the Mind. It's the mind which gives instructions to all body parts to do their respective work and functions appropriately.

I have a question for you Vinod. We both visited the **Graveyard** and **Post Mortem Ward**. What did you observe there?

Vinod: I saw a body which was brought by a couple of people and that body was not functioning. The people did some rituals. In some graveyards they then burned the body and in some graveyards they buried the body under the soil.

Dinesh: You mean to say, the body which is not functioning is the one that we call a **"Dead Body"** which is brought by a couple of people, whereas there are a couple of people whose existence is based on their body which is functioning, and we call it a **"Live Body"**. Could you tell me the difference between "Dead Body" and "Live Body"?

Vinod: The Live body will interact with its body parts and the body parts will interact with natural elements and natural resources. But the Dead body does not interact with anything.

Dinesh: Are body parts controlled by anything or not? If yes then how is the body working?

Vinod: As I understand and experience it, the body parts are controlled by one thing, we call it "**Mind**". The body works by communicating with other body parts.

Dinesh: Let me give you more clarification on body and mind. The body gets instructions from the brain which is a physical organ. But there is a metaphysical thing controlling the brain, that we call "Mind". It doesn't have size or shape and cannot be touched. The mind is the most important part of the body. As I understand and experience it, the body parts are controlled by one thing, we call it "Mind".

We often use the terms 'brain' and 'mind' interchangeably. The brain is a physical and tangible part. The mind is the activity centre of the brain. All the information processing done by the brain is called Mind. Using a laptop as an analogy, the brain is the hardware and the mind is a software.

In a laptop, the hardware determines how well the software is run. Similarly, the wiring of the brain will determine the state of our mind. The reverse is also true. The mind changes the brain structure. The information (mind) flowing through the brain is continuously sculpting our brain. So all the interactions and the inner dialogue we have are changing our brain and the changed brain structure influences our mind.

There is one more question. Is that process of interconnection between all body parts and mind controllable or uncontrollable?

Vinod: Some body parts are controllable and other body parts are uncontrollable.

Dinesh: Can you elaborate that?

Vinod: There are some body parts which are visible outside i.e. external side of body, which are controllable with limited time &

limited things. But other body parts which are inside are not controllable.

Dinesh: You said some body parts are controllable; who is the controller then?

Vinod: Of course it's the mind that controls it.

Dinesh: If mind controls it then it should be a common process to all human beings, right? So why are all the people not capable of controlling it then?

Vinod: It's not like that. Some human beings are capable of controlling it and some human beings are not capable of controlling it.

Dinesh: It means some are able to control and some are not. But how are some people controlling it? Is there anything that they are doing to control it?

Vinod: As you said, during our visit to the **Museum**, I have observed the achievements and awards of people who are common people but they have ambitions and goals, and they are determined to achieve them. They do hard work and smart work in the right direction to achieve the goals. To achieve anything, people have to work on body level and mind level. Firstly, they understand their own capability and the strengths and weaknesses of their body and mind then accordingly they work on this to master things that are required to achieve their goals.

Dinesh: Who trains the body and its parts along with the mind?

Vinod: It's Human beings who train the body parts and mind which will help them to achieve what they want. But the mind will help them control body parts and work with it.

Dinesh: It means that a human being controls both, the body parts and the mind to make decisions to do required things and he instructs his body parts through his mind. Can I say that the mind and the body parts work with each other to keep human beings alive?

Vinod: Yes, in order to live, human beings both mind and body should work with each other.

Dinesh: If one fails then human beings will die. We saw that at the **Mental Hospital,** right?

Vinod: No, there are some body parts which are crucial and some are non-crucial. The same applies to the mind. For outside physical parts if any part is not there and it's not a vital part then the body still works but it is important that vital internal organs work. As for the mind, its working, in case of any issues, will depend on the functionality of the missing part.

Dinesh: Are there physically handicapped people, who can also do all things that other human beings who have all body parts do?

Vinod: Disabled people can also do the same things but in different ways as per the determination. If they try to use their parts on a daily basis to do that activity then one day they will be able to do it. These people use their body parts creatively in a way that no one can imagine because others do it the normal way because they do not have any such physical difficulty.

Many physically disabled people do all the things based on their willingness and trust in themselves that they can achieve it. It also applies to mentally challenged people. It also depends on the person.

This all depends on what they think and what they want from life. The people who want to do something, they will work on it until it is done. If the reason why they want to achieve it, is very strong emotionally and it is to help mankind, then they can change the things around them.

Dinesh: Can human beings control all the things that the mind does to its body parts?

Vinod: No, not all, only a few things. Internal body parts like vital organs are not in our control but external body parts which are visible can be controlled. We can give instructions to external body parts based on the requirements.

Dinesh: Do you know about consciousness & subconsciousness of mind?

Vinod: Yes, I know. **Consciousness** - If human beings do any new things or do old things in new ways, at that time they are conscious of what they are doing with complete focus, attention and concentration because the activity will be new to the mind and body parts. They are completely active and aware of what they are doing. But when it comes to **Subconsciousness,** it is the activity that is done by mind and body parts without human being's active involvement. It's as though body parts automatically do it themselves because it has been done many times hence the body and mind remember its patterns and it can be done automatically.

For Example: From morning to night, the day-to-day activities that we do, like eating, cooking, habits, walking, talking, working, keyboard typing, driving bike and car, swimming, writing, reading, using devices and things, sleeping, happen unconsciously because our mind and body parts are aware of it.

Is this what you want to know or do you want to say something from a different perspective?

Dinesh: This is what I want to know and Addition to that, The moment we consciously do things at each and every moment, awarely with complete focus and attention, we shall live the present moment which makes us experience the aliveness of human life.

If we are completely aware and conscious of day-to-day activities that we do then we can pause during our activities or do things in different ways to be aware of the present moment. This is very important to experience life, to live in the present moment, to instruct the mind as well as the body parts to do things which are controllable & to give commands to the mind which, in turn, will give commands to body parts.

Example: Count the steps when we walk; completely concentrate while eating from the plate to cheve, make eye contact while talking, to experience the liveliness of human beings in their eyes and to live in the present moment.

Once people start to experience and live in the present moment then their way of living will change, such that they are aware of each and every moment and experience life. This way they live and experience every day differently but others live and experience every day the same way.

Was your query about how to live in the present moment addressed?

Vinod: It was addressed clearly and I will try my level best to live in the present moment.

About Realization and Satisfaction

Dinesh: There are certain things I wanted to be clear about, with regard to realization and satisfaction. Once people live in the present moment then they realize & are satisfied with the things that they have. These people will provide their gratitude for what they have. There is a huge difference between realization of and satisfaction with the things that we have and the things that we don't have. People will identify which of these are very necessary to live human life.

About Realization: When people want to do anything in life then they will take help of other human beings or devices to complete the required task or activity or work. At that time they do not realize the importance of that person or device but when they want to do the same thing again and the person or device is not there at that time, they realize the importance of that person or thing.
As for a device, you can get a new one because it is created by human beings so there is no need to worry.
But as for human beings, they are nature's creation. Once a person leaves, there is no way to get him back. Hence after losing a person, many people realize the importance of that person in life.
But true realization is understanding the importance of that person when they are together and alive.

About Satisfaction: Whenever people are doing any work or activity or hobby, they do that activity to the point where others can also say that the work is completed and that they can now stop. But that person knows whether it is completed or missing something. If they experience incompleteness, then they see there is still something which is missing because they think, "**I am not**

satisfied with this and I can take it to a level which nobody has done or imagined". In many situations people have to do that activity only to the point of completion, due to time limit, resource limit, lack of interest, etc. If they take that thing to the next level then they call it a "**Masterpiece**" which nobody has done or imagined.

Vinod: Could you elaborate about realizing the importance of a person?

Dinesh: When you live with a person, give your complete attention & focus to that person with love and happiness. Every person looks for love and happiness to enjoy life but they often don't get it, due to which they look for it in other things like Devices and Other species which are temporary and have time limit.

Follow the Instructions and Experience it yourself

Vinod: How to give complete attention, focus, love & happiness?
Dinesh: Do you know emotions are part of human life? Instead of telling you, I want you to try what I am instructing, and experience it for the next one week because you can understand it only when you experience it, then you will share your experience and we will continue later.

Instructions to experience emotions:
1. Keep eye contact whenever you are in contact with human beings.
2. Try to help people whenever necessary, with or without their knowing that you are helping them. If the person is a stranger, then ask, "Is it fine if I help you?" Otherwise, if you know the person, you can help them directly.
3. Make sure compassion, love, happiness flow through your actions to other people via expressions & emotions.
4. Emotions have to flow so beware when what flows through you is anger, ego, depression, anxiety, jealousy, etc. When you are angry, don't reply at that time. Be aware of the present moment when your emotions flow then you will automatically understand what you need to do at that time. But I will still suggest you note the following information. Anger: Not to reply at that time; be calm and accept. Ego: It is more important than life. Depression & Anxiety : Realize everything you have, and also why you need not worry about the things that you don't have. Jealousy: Do I really require it so much that I can't live without it?
5. Your body & mind should be in your control. Don't give it to others to control it with their actions. You need to be completely aware of what you are doing. If necessary, try to train your body

and mind. If you have any issues then learn from them and never repeat the same mistakes.

6. Whatever is there inside you, it will come outside through actions. It will flow through emotions, thoughts, feelings, love, happiness and smiles. Make sure to be aware of what is within you, by spending time with yourself.

7. Fundamental: Human beings come with empty hands and go with empty hands, so remain aware of this fact.

8. Devices can be created again, but human beings cannot. Give importance to human beings rather than to devices. Because devices are there to be used, not to love, while human beings are there to be loved, not to be used. Most of the times, people love devices and use humans.

9. Live in the present moment.

10. Don't do anything that makes others dependent on you; help them to realize their potential to do things independently.

Follow these instructions and then let me know. I have some work so I will be out for a week then I will meet you next week at the temple. But make sure that next week you have happiness & love, replete with beautiful, life-changing memories, to remember lifelong.

Vinod: Okay, sure. I will do as you said and meet you next week at the temple.
We met at the temple after one week.

Dinesh: Share with me, your experience for this one week.
Vinod: Previously, I used to talk to people without eye contact so I couldn't remember the face and emotions of that person. But when I started making eye contact while talking, I realized and experienced the liveliness of human beings. The moment I made eye contact, I was present at that moment and giving complete

focus and attention to that person. Now when we both talk to each other, we are in the present moment. Because the moment another person misses eye contact, he is thinking of something about the past or imagining about the future while talking. This eye contact makes me realize, people always live in the past or future because they always do things without being aware of the present moment. It's as though they are running through the journey of life without stopping & looking at life experiences.

Later when I visited my place, it felt like I was there with my family for the first time because when I went inside the house, I saw my mom and was able to talk to her by keeping eye contact. My mom also maintained eye contact for a long time, which made me realize that I had not been able to give attention to my mom for these many days. Earlier, I used to speak to my mom but we had eye contact very rarely. Spending time with my mom over a couple of days made me realize that I gave my complete attention, focus, love, care & happiness. In case my mom wasn't there at the next moment i.e. if she were to die, I wouldn't have any regrets & I would be happy that I spent time with my mom. It made me realize that people miss these things due to which they have complaints and regrets of missing their near and dear ones.

The most important thing which I have thought of is that every person who takes birth on this planet has to leave one day but when I visited the **Graveyard,** I realized people always miss other persons after losing them as they could not spend time with them due to a lack of the habit of living in the present moment. They always spend time with that person but not with attention & focus due to which they are not able to experience their presence while communicating and living together. I realized most of the times people always realize the importance of that person after they die. At that time they say, "I could have spent time with you." but it's not their mistake because they are always running without thinking about what they are doing and why they are doing it.

Some are running towards getting financial stability for their family, to survive a good standard of life but forgetting they can live with the things that they have if they understand the difference between need and greed. I realized human beings look for love, happiness & pleasure in one way or the other in what they are doing but are not able to give it to others due to responsibilities that they have to fulfill for their family. Due to the lack of realization & satisfaction of what they have, they always run behind what they don't have & miss out on living life with what they have – both devices and people.

Forgetting To Realize That Devices Can Be Remade or Repurchased but Not Human Beings

The other day, when I was going to the temple, I saw that villagers had gathered so I went there. I asked some people what was happening; they said, a boy was missing since yesterday so they were worried. I asked them whether anything had happened before he went missing. The boy's mother said that his father shouted at him & beat him because he broke some device. Before that also, every time he made any mistake or broke anything, his father always shouted at him and beat him. I saw his father and said, "Do you know what you did? You are not understanding your son. If he did any mistake or anything, you need to understand whether he is doing it by mistake or something is wrong with him. If you could spend some time with him to understand him then that would not happen in this situation. He is a child not mature enough to understand things." Later the father realized that he could not spend time in understanding him but he always worried & worked for them only. I said, "Don't worry. I will find him and bring him home. I have started searching for him by getting more information from his friends, and asked my friends, neighbors and other villagers." After 2 hours I got a call from my friends specifying they found him in the city. I went there and we both sat at the hotel to eat as he was hungry. We completed our lunch. I started explaining to the boy, "Listen, your parents are working day and night for you. Make sure you don't hurt them any further. If you have any problem then come to me; we will discuss and resolve it. I talked to your father, he will never beat and shout at you." We came back and I handed the boy to his parents.

Dinesh: What did you realize about this incident?

Vinod: People give more importance to devices or things than people and keep "**forgetting to realize that devices can be remade or repurchased but not human beings**". Once they die or something very bad happens between them then they will never forget it and that leads to breaking of relationships due to misunderstanding and miscommunication.

There is another incident which taught me many things. This happened when I visited my father for some work. He was thinking about something and seemed to be worried. I could sense that while I was talking to him. I asked him, "What happened, Father? Is everything alright?"

Father: No, there is a man in our village, who is an old friend of mine. His name is Rajayya. He has 2 sons & 2 daughters. They are facing some challenges regarding property. They used to live happily until his children's marriages. But since their marriage, they have some misunderstanding between them and now everybody is living separately and nowadays no one is talking to each other in their family. The parents tried to talk to their children to settle things between them. But they are not ready to listen to their parents. We already have some panchayats to discuss and finalize things among them but today evening they have a final **Panchayat** to divide the property equally between them so that they can live happily without any issues. ("Panchayat" is the name we use for the village council where we discuss village issues and meetings).

Vinod: After distributing the property, will they live happily, talk to each other as they used to before marriage, and keep their mother and father happy?

Father: I think they will talk to each other when there is a need or emergency but still there would be no love and respect for each other.

Vinod: How to make them back to normal as usual so that they can live happily after the distribution of the property?

Father: I think I know what to do with them so that they can live happily.

Vinod: Tell me what you are going to do, Father. What is the plan or idea?

Father: There is one story, which I want to tell them all during our Panchayat. Later let them decide what they want to do.

Vinod: In the evening, we all gathered. My father started a Panchayat.

Father: We all gathered here today evening to distribute the property of Rajayya among his 4 children. As we all already have listened to his children, we tried to convince them to understand and forgive each other, and forget any issues or problems they have among themselves so that they can live happily, support each other, love and live happily. They all agreed to these conditions that they would support, love, forget their issues and forgive each other but still they requested the distribution of the property among them while their father is alive otherwise this will lead to more problems and conflicts in the future if the property is not distributed now. As I see, their point of view is also valid so I discussed with Rajayya and distributed the property in 4 equal parts as the children agreed to distribute equal parts to each of them, irrespective of whether it's a son or a daughter. Their father has some property and money in his account to live independently till he dies. He can live with any son or daughter family for as long as wishes. Later that property belonging to him will be donated to the village for development as all agreed to it. Every portion of the property will be distributed and registered as per the children's names so that there will be no conflict related to the property in the future. Before I hand over the registered documents and complete this Panchayat, I want to tell you one story so that you can all decide whether you give more importance to values, roles, or responsibilities.

Story:

Everyone is Important and Responsible

This is the story of a single person and how he made the entire village his family.
Character Names: Srinivas, Laxmi, Venkata, Doctor, Saraswati and Yashwant.

Srinivas & Laxmi are a married couple. It's an arranged marriage. Venkata is their child. One day, Srinivas & Laxmi went to the hospital for polio vaccine dose to Venkata. After completing the polio dose, the doctor called both Srinivas & Laxmi.
Doctor: Are you both planning for any more children?
Laxmi: Yes, we are planning for 2 more children.
Doctor: Okay, There is something I want to share with you which I kept secret, waiting for the right moment. I think now it's the right time. During Venkata's birth, we observed that Laxmi's uterus got an infection. The womb, also called uterus, is where a fetus (unborn baby) develops and grows. We tried to remove the infection from the uterus but it was too late. At that time, Venkata and Laxmi's safety was more important to us. If we made any mistake then both Venkata and Laxmi's life would be at risk and the infection could spread to Venkata also. we doctors decided to remove Laxmi's uterus without informing you. We wanted to tell you at that time only but you would not have accepted and understood it, so we decided to tell you later when the time was right. I think, now you are in a position to understand what we did to save both lives at that time.

Srinivas: Laxmi, don't cry. I am happy that you and Venkata both are safe. Thank you Doctor for taking a good decision and informing us at the right time.

Doctor: There are many such cases that have happened here, but there is one incident, which helped me to understand that the relationship between parents and children can be gone to any extent.

Let me share with you the story of "Saraswati":
There was a pregnant woman who came for delivery. We delivered the baby successfully and it was a boy. The parents were very happy. After 2 years, the woman came again for the test as she was planning for her next child. We tested her and found that her uterus has had problems after her 1st birth. The uterus cannot support a baby anymore. She cried at the beginning but later she was happy that at least she had 1 child. They both left for the day. A year later, I was going to a village for a relative's function, passing through a vegetable market. While I was going, I saw a baby girl crying in the middle of the market and saying, "Teacher, teacher." I went to the baby and cooed at her, asking her not to cry. I asked around about the baby and whether anybody knew any teacher. I asked the vegetable sellers. They said, "We know this baby and the teacher's home is near that tree." I went to the tree and asked about the teacher. They pointed to a house. When I went there, a voice came from inside, "Aaradhya, again you went to the market. I told you to play here only, right?" When I saw that person, it was an old patient of mine and her name was Saraswati. She saw and greeted me.

Saraswati: Hello Doctor, how are you? It's been a long time.

Doctor: Hello Saraswati, I am good. Yes, it's been a long time. How are you?

Saraswati: I am good.

Doctor: How is your son?

Saraswati: There was an incident that happened 6 months after we met last time and he didn't survive. He died in that incident.

Doctor: I am really sorry. Could you please tell me exactly what incident happened?

Saraswati: Yes sure, as a doctor you can at least intimate your patients early.

For the better future of our son, we moved to a nearby city. My husband looked for a new job. I am a housewife and was only taking care of my son. The location which we chose in the city was good, as compared to other locations. After 2 months, it was the rainy season. We observed that during the rainy season there is immense clogging of rain water in roads and houses after heavy rains. One day, we went to the hospital for our son's checkup. The taxi reached halfway. The driver said, "Ma'am we cannot go any further because of yesterday's heavy rains. The road is not constructed well so it has holes due to which the water has blocked the road and clogged the drainage. More and more water is getting clogged on the streets. Please go on foot from here and be careful." While we were going to the hospital, we observed one person removing all the garbage which blocked the drainage. We went to the hospital. After the checkup, when we returned from the hospital there was heavy rain. When we were walking on the same road, the same person we had seen earlier was wearing a raincoat and still removing the garbage from the drainage. My husband went to him and thanked him for cleaning. He smiled and said, "Thank you, my son." We both went home. After 2 weeks, we observed that some mosquitoes started coming to our houses in the evening. When I discussed with my neighbors whether there were mosquitoes here, they all said, "Yes, every year during the rainy season we also observe the same thing. One reason behind this is the water blockage present in our surroundings for a long time." We arranged nets around our house & windows and used Mosquito Killer Machine & Coils to prevent mosquito bites. We observed, day by day in our society, children and adults were getting malaria even though they were taking precautions. One day, I was going to the market and observed the same person distributing mosquito coils freely and there was a board around his neck, **"Please throw garbage into the dustbin only and keep all your surroundings clean"**. I was shocked at first. Why would anybody go to this extent to clean drainage, distribute coils and more importantly, place a board around his neck? Somebody next to me said to another person, "Again this old person has come the same way he does every year, doing all these things for the entire rainy season." While I was leaving the market, the old person was not there. I went home. After 2 months, our son got malaria. We went to the hospital and moved to different hospitals for better treatment but his condition became critical. In one hospital, he got better. We came home. After 1 week, suddenly his condition became serious. We were on our way to the hospital but there was a sudden traffic jam due to the accident of a car and a bus. We got passage to get out of the traffic. We were about to enter into the hospital but our son suddenly fell unconscious. We were worried and handed over our son to the doctors. The doctors did the treatment and after some time, they came out and said, "We are sorry. Your son died." We both cried. The doctors said his body was too weak internally after treatment. We both did his funeral and returned to our hometown. One day, I went to a temple to pray for my son. Over there I saw a person with a board on his neck **"Please give me some work as I don't speak"**. It reminded me of that old person I had seen. I thought, "I will also do the same thing to keep other children safe." I went to the city, as I was curious to know **why he was doing all these things.** Did he also go through something? When I enquired about him, I got his address. I went to his address and met him. I said, "My name is Saraswati & I saw you clean the drainage, distribute coils and more importantly, keep board around your neck with suggestions. I am curious about this. **Why are you doing all these things?** Recently, I lost my son. I am also doing the same thing to make others aware of these things. Did you too experience a similar incident? " He said, "My name is **Yashwant**. Yes, a similar incident happened which changed our lives. Only we can understand why I am doing this. You look like my daughter; I have been doing this for the last 7 years but nobody has come and asked me the reason. I am happy at least you want to know the reason. I will tell you everything; at least you will get a warning in advance. 7 years ago, I was living happily with my son, daughter in law, grandson and granddaughter. My grandson and granddaughter were both infected by malaria. My granddaughter was older so she survived but my grandson died. We took all precautions but still we were unable to save him. My son and I loved him so much. We decided to understand the root cause of malaria to prevent children from getting malaria and dying. We visited local areas and did a survey in hospitals. We found that many children die because of malaria. When we analyzed and observed after a couple of months, we observed that in the rainy season many cases get registered and 10% of children die every year. We found the root cause of it as **"Everybody's carelessness leads to this"**. We observed that people are not disposing their garbage into the dustbin. Instead of that they throw it anywhere. For example, if one person throws it in the corner of the road, then all start throwing there and some throw garbage into the dustbin from a distance as though trying to score a goal, and all garbage is spilled outside dustbin. All the garbage is collected like a dump. If the garbage is there outside for more than 1 week then mosquitos and other insects get life. During the rainy season all garbage goes into drainages and it blocks water. If water is blocked in drainage places for more time then again, mosquitos and other insects get life. Everybody keeps their home clean but nobody wants to keep their society or area clean.

Everybody is running for their survival and future, and is too busy in their life. During meetings in our society or areas they all talk about cleaning the drainage and garbage but nobody comes and cleans anything. The government cleaners only clean and remove garbage which is visible to all till a particular time in the morning upto some extent. The remaining areas kept as it is and they generate all insects. The roads are also not built properly and after a couple of months, they start developing holes in them. It leads to accidents and water blockage on roads in the rainy season. It leads to the birth of insects. Nobody comes from home to clean roads. During the rainy season, the government servants try their level best to keep things clean but they lack equipment and this should be planned in advance. For example: 2 months before the rainy season, all drainages should be clear so that water can flow without logging. All the roads should be constructed and there should be no holes. All low-lying places where there was water logging last time should be built well so that they cannot be water-logged anymore. Every society should respond to it and take all these concerns to a respected person who is in charge and accountable for all these things. Many people do not have time for themselves and their own family, so how can they fight for all these things? Even if somebody or society takes all these things to the right person, they only ask us to give an application and tell us they will do it. But in reality they don't do it. The society has to follow up multiple times and they don't have any escalation matrix which clearly states if the person does not do this in this particular time then it will escalate to his superior automatically. If the superior does not take any action, then it will escalate to higher management. The superiors get penalty or punishment or resignation based on issue type and priority. If any in-charge wants to do it but he has lack of resources and budget for it because there is no transparency of funds or resources, nobody is ready to ask about the fund details or nobody is responsible to show the funding details to the respective society. Society can be anywhere in a village or city.

The funds and resources allocated by governments to respective Ward's or branches for each village or city should be available and should be declared in advance at the time of allocation of funds and resources by the government. Everything should be kept transparent, right from allocation to use of all resources by proper approvals and verifications by the local public. Then only our country can develop young generations into leaders by saving all children.

My son and I tried to convince our society about these things but nobody cares and they don't have time for all these things. We approached the in-charge. He asked us to give an application or register a complaint. We did that and asked him how much time it would take. He said he could not assure you of time as it depends on many factors. We gave applications but nothing changed in our society. After a month we again went to that in-charge but he was busy and after 5 times of going to his office, we found it was still in progress and it would take more time. After 2 months, there was still no change in our society. When we went again, we didn't find any response. We tried to meet his superior but he also did the same thing. When we tried his superior the same thing happened. When we approached the media about it, nobody responded. We don't have any support and resources to approach the court. After 1 year, my son and I decided that nobody responded. We both decided on our own to start cleaning drainages, distribute coils and more importantly, wear boards on our neck without listening to others because we know the pain of my grandson but they don't. We want them to keep their children safe as children are children, whether their own or others'. We did that for 3 years, and the next year my son died in a road accident. My son was driving very carefully by taking all precautions and following all the rules but the opposite person was driving faster than the declared rules.

They both collided and my son fell in the opposite direction and the vehicle went into his body and he died while he was being taken into hospital. After 1 year, his wife also died because of health issues as we couldn't afford her treatment in big hospitals. Now I follow those things and I take care of my granddaughter. I am only worried about what will happen to my granddaughter after I die. This is all the reason behind those things.

Saraswati: I can totally understand what you have been going through all this time. Don't worry. As you said, I am like your daughter. I will take care of you and your granddaughter by staying here.

I convinced my husband and we both stayed there. I used to teach Aaradhya. Later all children in the society came to me for tuition. One day, I was crying while looking at my son's photo. Suddenly, my father, Yashwant came and said.

Yashwant: Don't cry, my daughter. As you are teaching all these children, why don't you see your son in all of them? They all are innocent. You can treat all of them like your children. You love all of them in every possible way by taking care of them, playing with them, teaching them and helping them if they have any difficulties. **"Encourage them to ask questions because then only they will start thinking on their own and grow by finding answers to it"**. But always remember one thing, **"Don't expect anything from anyone. This applies to the present and the future"**. Give all you've got. **Be true to yourself and with them**. If they ask anything, then say clearly if you know about it, otherwise say, "I don't know. I will get information & knowledge about it and let you know." If you lie then that information & knowledge will be used in future and they'll take support of that data which will lead them in the wrong direction. In general, if you lie to anyone by hiding the truth then without any control, you will continue lying one after the other to hide the truth. You will always have a fear that if that person came to know the truth, then it would be a problem for you. Because of that you are unable to stay calm and sleep well because you know you are lying. Please tell the truth and explain the circumstances which made you do that, so that other people can forgive you by understanding your perspective and situation. That's why I told you to say the same thing to them, that is, **"Be true to yourself"**. Teach everything you got.

Saraswati: Thank you, Father. I will find my son in all of them, love and enjoy with them as though I am also a kid. **I will be true to myself and ask them to be true to themselves.**

Yashwant: There is one more suggestion I want to give you if you are willing to give a try to implement it.

Saraswati: Yes, Father. Please tell me.

Yashwant: In the beginning, I used to live with my parents in a village. We all were living happily. The villagers were very happy and very helpful. All of us were living happily with what we had and what we did. One of the families of my village went to the city for their children's bright future and settled down in the city. They kept their parents in the village as they were not used to living in the city. They loved to live in villages only. Thereon, one by one, the families in the village started to move to the city for their children's bright future. Some parents went with them to the city and some stayed in the village only. Only a few people in the village were left. In the city, both parents or a single parent started working and they didn't get to spend time and talk to their children after work. Once the children were adults, they grew up with their friends of the same age who were mostly immature because all they wanted is a comfortable life with all the accessories that they required or other children had. The parents who could afford it, bought it and others had to struggle a lot. Their children didn't think about their current situation and financial condition. Once the accessories were bought, they didn't think about how those accessories came, and whether that was required or not. Very few children used what they had, whether that was an accessory or some other thing, whereas the rest of them kept it unused and looked for different accessories. During this time, the bond that should develop between parents and children does not develop the way it used to. Because of this, children don't understand their parents and vice versa. When the children get married they understand that becoming a parent is not a simple thing. Then they relate to everything about how their parents worked so hard and both, the children and the parents weren't able to give much love, value, time and respect to each other. Now the same thing is happening with their children. But here their children also look for their children's bright future and very few children care about their parents. The rest all live their life by leaving parents who are not in their control, even if they want to live together, due to a lack of understanding between parents and married children. They both want their privacy. In some time, the parents become old and they become like babies and here their children turn to take care of them but at this time their children are unable to balance their current and future plans, work and taking care of their children. Here mostly the parents want to spend their time with their children and children also want to spend their time with their parents by taking care of them but the circumstances are such that the parents expect support and care from their children but it is not fulfilled because of these things. Parents and children break internally due to lack of communication between them, wherein they both expect each other to understand their respective situations and circumstances and live the rest of their life on their own. There are some situations where both misunderstand each other, being unaware of applying the principle of "Forget and Forgive" to fix things and restart things. This is what happens between parents and children where they both understand things when things are out of hand but at that time it's too late.

The solution for these things is to understand that blood relations cannot be chosen; they always happen without any choice. Most of the times, problems and misunderstandings happen because both people are right from their own point of view because no one tells them that they were wrong and should accept it and say sorry. Both sides should sit together and discuss things clearly; one or both sides should apologize for their mistakes and others should accept the mistake and then go back to their normal state. They can also apply the principle of **"Forget and Forgive"**. **Forget** things which have happened in the past i.e. a second ago or a minute ago or an hour ago or a day ago or a week ago or a month ago or a year ago or years ago. There is no use in remembering it and keeping it with us, instead of understanding why those things or issues happened and finding their root cause so that this cannot be repeated in the future. **Forgive** those people or things which happened knowingly or unknowingly due to immaturity or misunderstanding. A simple example of this is, **"What is more important? A relationship or an issue?"** Most of the times, a relationship is more important, no matter whether it is within a family or between families or friends or neighbors or colleagues or even strangers. It is also important to understand that we should take care those who are with us right now. Otherwise we will think of and remember them after they die. We don't care about the beloved person who is with us right now. This way if that person also dies then we do the same thing. Instead of that, we should understand and accept the people's death, and spend enough time with the remaining people who are with us right now. One more thing which stops people from going beyond their limits is that they set and define limits for people and things in their mind. Example: These are my family or friends or neighbors or colleagues and this much is my home or house or building or village or city or state or country or world. Once these limits are removed mentally, and we give respect, value, help, love and compassion to every being whether it is a human being or any other being without any expectations by understanding their point of view from a different perspective, then everyone will live happily by supporting each other because "**Everyone is important because of their roles and responsibilities**". The roles and responsibilities could be official or unofficial or in relations, etc. If you apply the above things in your family then everyone will live happily by supporting each other in difficult times. Here, "Family" means not just your family; it means your entire society or village or city or country or world or planet. I would suggest you to think big, start smaller and then extend.

My old generations transferred this to me and now I am passing this on to you. It helped me a lot of times and I applied this in many ways. There are some of my friends who also told me that it helped them. Please tell this story to others so that it can reach those who require it.

Saraswati: Yes, Father. I will apply this wherever it is possible and I will also share this to others so that it helps them.

From my father's story, one thing was clear to me. The people who live in the city are very busy with their present and future plans so they are not ready to change anything. The children also become busy with their requirements and education. Then I saw there is hope in villagers to adapt and change themselves. I decided to visit my native village and give tuitions to village children and start implementing what makes me and others, better human beings. I moved to my native village.

Now this village is my family. I shared this story to the people of the village so that they understand, "**Everyone is Important and Responsible**". I Always help the people by understanding their problems and their point of view. Then we discuss this in such a way that I ask them counter questions and they give answers which opens their mind towards thinking what's right and where they are wrong. Later they accept they are wrong and correct themselves. Most of the times when anyone is facing a problem or challenge, they come to me and I give my time to solve their issues. I also ask them to, counter question themselves when they are in trouble because I will not be there forever. It makes me happy that I helped them.

This is the incident that happened and it changed my life, Doctor.

Doctor: Thank you Saraswati. I will also apply this and share it with others so that it can reach out to all those people who require it.

This is the story, Srinivas & Laxmi, that I applied and shared to all those who required it so that it helps them to understand that the relationship between parents and children can be up to any extent to fulfill roles and responsibilities because everyone is important. Before it's too late to apply the "Forget and Forgive" Principle, both children and parents should give each other enough time to discuss everything. This is all I want to share with you.

Srinivas & Laxmi: Thank you Doctor. We understand very well and we will also share it.

They both said goodbye to each other.

Father: This is the story which I want to tell you, to decide what is more important to you based on your priorities: values, roles and responsibilities.

The above story, I heard from my friend and I applied this many times, especially the **"Forget and Forgive"** Principle. I also applied the funds and resources allocated to this village in a very precise manner by thinking about **"What is more important"** and **"Thinking about current and future problems in advance at root level"**. I used to keep the Funds and resources with transparency for village members so that I could build **"Trust & Love"** between all so that we all live happily and support each other in difficult times. Most importantly **"I Always think of this village as my family."**; this way, I can understand what they want, in advance, without getting to knowing from them directly. Spend enough time with the people who are with us right now instead of crying after they die, once it's too late.

I hope this story helps all of you and please share it with those who require it.

Now I handed over the registered documents to Rajayya and his children. The Panchayat was over.

Vinod: This is the story which helped me a lot, Dinesh.

Dinesh: I think this one week taught you lessons that will help you to become mature enough to understand things from another person's perspective.

If you see any problem then there are multiple ways to solve the problem but the important thing is to understand why that problem arises & from where. Does this problem have some meaning or lesson that I want to learn? How to fix these problems permanently? How many people are affected by the problem at different levels i.e. at personal, professional, family & societal levels? How to solve the problem in the best and most efficient way by utilizing the resources we have? These are the things I want you to keep in mind while facing any problem or challenge.

About Dinesh's Journey

Now, you wanted to know about me and my details, like where I am from and what I am doing here, right?

Vinod: Yes, I am very eager to know about you.

Dinesh: Now, I think it's time to tell you about my journey. I live in **Mumbai** in the state of **Maharashtra, India**. I was born there in a middle-class background. My dad is a car driver in a private company and my mom is a maid. I am the eldest child and I have 1 brother and 1 sister. We are 5 members in a family. My father is uneducated but he has good skills to complete outside work and help others. His wish is to educate us so that we can be independent. He never forced us to do anything; he always said, "Just go for what you want but make sure before deciding that this is what you want, and understand why you want it. Once your reason is strong enough then you will automatically work for it. In some cases, you want to do things without any reason, and that's fine but stay true to yourself. Let me know if you need any help from my side." My dad helped me a lot and I always get clarity on what I'm doing and why I am doing it.

I completed my schooling and I was 17 years old when I joined college for 11th and 12th standard in the Science Stream. I completed my 11th and for 12th I joined a coaching class which was run by our college professors with nominal fees. The professor's motto was to help middle- and low-income background students to get good grades so that they can take care of their family in future. In my academics, I had many doubts so I was able to ask some in class and some outside class. Some professors appreciated me for asking doubts in class and some students made fun of me. During class I used to do a lot of fun, jokes and comedy, and enjoyed myself. This started when I was in 11th grade. One professor caught me while cracking jokes and having fun. He gave me the punishment of standing on the bench. It reminded me of an old incident which happened during school time. I had received the same punishment but while getting up and going to stand on the bench my shorts were stuck to the chair and people saw me without shorts. All the students and even the teacher laughed. Thereafter whenever I stood on the bench all the students in the class started to laugh. I remembered this incident and started laughing while the professor was giving me a punishment. The professor asked me why I was laughing then I shared this incident with all of them. All the students & the professor started laughing. Later the professor appreciated me for laughing at my own incidents. During class, my professors used to take me as an example whenever they wanted to explain any concept. All class members started to enjoy and laugh. One professor made fun of me and later, outside the class, he said, "Sorry. I used to take your examples to explain concepts because the moment I take your examples, class members are happy and active. So please don't mind it." For that, I said, "You are always welcome, sir. Those are my friends; some talk and some don't talk but still they are all my friends. I am very happy because they are all happy and enjoying it. Seeing this makes me happy." I realised, "This college days are golden days of life which never come back in life". I want to enjoy each and every moment with all of them because even if we planned, we didn't unite or get this many friends for this many years in future. Sir said, "You are something different & good; keep it up." I asked, "Sir, something different? I didn't understand that." Sir said, "Don't worry, you will understand when it's time." At that time, I said okay and we left for the day. Next day, I had doubts about all the subjects that I was studying. Where did they use these subjects? I visited the professor's room during the break and asked the same question.

For that one professor said, "Every subject is used in real life". For example, Chemistry is for creating colors using chemicals and using them in shirts and all clothes. Biology is to make medicines. Maths is for calculation to create blueprints for Buildings. Physics for understanding things around us and creating equations to calculate speed, time and velocity. These are only the basics but when you go for graduation and masters, you'll understand better. I told him I got the answers and left for lunch. In the class, the most enjoyable period was lunch time where all my friends in different batches sat together and shared each other's tiffin. I tasted all different kinds of food and I loved it.

About Kanchana and The Promise

I also enjoyed and waited for the lunch period because there was a girl in a different batch whom I liked and I enjoyed talking to her. Whenever I saw her face and smile since our first meeting, it made me feel joyful, happy and stunned at the same time. I got the opportunity to meet that girl and share tiffin. So, every lunch period, we all friends enjoyed sharing our tiffin & I also talked to that girl as a friend because I didn't share my feelings with her. It had been 6 months. One day during the lunch period, we all friends gathered in different batches and had lunch. I noticed the girl was missing. So after lunch we came to our class. The next day also, that girl was missing so I was worried because she never missed a single class and I thought maybe she had some health issue or had gone out with her family. I asked my other friends about her, "Why is she not coming?" They said that she was not well. I said Okay. After a couple of days, I was in class when another professor came in between & informed our professor that a girl of another batch had died. The class ended early and all the professors collected some money and went to that girl's house. I went outside class and asked one of our friends about who had died. They said, "It's **Kanchana**". I was shocked and collapsed. It was the girl who I loved. I was not in a position to talk to anyone. I was quiet and completely silent, able to listen to my own heartbeat. Our lunchtime friends decided to visit her place. So, we all went to her house by taxi. When we went inside her house, everyone sat down. Some of our friends were crying and her mom was also crying. One of my friends asked her mom what happened.

Kanchana's Mom: She had blood cancer. She was in treatment for the past 4 months. She was ready to fight against cancer with proper treatment by taking medicines on time and weekly checkups. She was doing well till last week. She wanted to continue classes but we requested her to take rest. Till yesterday she was in good condition. We had dinner and we all went to our beds to sleep. She said, "Mom, you sleep next to me." I said OKAY. We both slept. In the middle of the night, she woke me up and said, "Mom, I love you." We both talked. After some time, she said, "I am going to the bathroom." She went there and came back. Again, she said, "I need to go to the bathroom." After a couple of minutes, I heard her vomiting. I was worried and went inside the bathroom. She hugged me and started crying. I asked her what happened. She was still crying. When I looked at the washbasin, there was blood all over the basin. I was shocked and worried. She said, "I vomited blood. I want to live; I don't want to die. Mom, I want to live. Please tell God I want to live." All our family members woke up and arranged for an ambulance. She hugged me tightly and cried, saying, "I want to live, Mom." I said, "Don't worry. Nothing will happen to you." After some time, she stopped talking and became unconscious. The ambulance came and after reaching the hospital, she was taken into the emergency ward. After some time, the doctor came outside, said, "She was in the last stage and we couldn't save her. She died." We all family members started crying. Today morning we did her cremation.

Dinesh: I saw Kanchana's picture which was in front of me, continuously for a long time without blinking. Deep within me I said to myself, **"I love you & I miss you so much Kanchana. I wanted to marry you."** I realized she wanted to live life but she died and at her last breath she was crying. I gave her a promise from deep within over there that I would really do something in my life so that **"People can realize and experience life when they live and on their last breath they can leave happily with a smile on their face"**. This is the **1st incident, which made me think and know more about life.** I was depressed for that 1st week and did not talk to any of our friends. They all started asking me what happened. I said I was not well and left from there. One day my neighbor also asked the same thing. His name was **Anand**. He was a very good person and helped me in my academics. I told him everything as I respected and trusted him.

Anand: Listen, Dinesh, I know how you are feeling but if Kanchana was alive, she would definitely want you to concentrate on Academics and get good grades in 12th so that she could be proud of you. You also made her a promise from deep within, right? You promised to find something in your life so that people can leave happily with a smile on their face.

Important Things About Teaching

Dinesh: Yes, you are right. From that day onwards, I concentrated on my studies. I got good results in 12th. I joined a good college for graduation in BSc IT as I got a good score in Maths. I was in my 1st year of graduation when I joined NSS in my college. It was free and we got 10 marks for it. **I love the word "Free"**. Whenever I see anything "Free" then I go there and get that thing. During my academic years, there was a teacher who was my favorite. Her name was **Poonam**. We all loved her and her lectures because she gave real life examples and the way she explained was very easy to understand. Mostly I asked her my queries related to the subject and beyond the subject.

One day, one of her lectures was over and the next lecture started but I was not able to understand anything. When I checked with my friends they also said that they didn't understand. During lunch break, I went to Ms.Poonam's staff room and said, "I want to ask you something."

Poonam Ma'am: Okay, but is it related to the subject or outside the subject?

Dinesh: It's a kind of personal question, beyond the subject.

Poonam Ma'am: Okay, we can take a walk around the campus and talk.

Dinesh: We both went outside the staff room and started walking around the campus.

Poonam Ma'am: Tell me your query.

Dinesh: There is a professor and I am not able to understand anything when she teaches. I asked some of my class friends and they also said the same thing. Only very few of them understand her teaching but we are able to understand your lectures very clearly. Why is it so, Ma'am?

Poonam Ma'am: The first thing is that we both are our own subject matter experts based on our love and passion for teaching but the following are the important things about teaching which I learnt over a period of time.

1. Understanding the students' level in that particular subject.
2. Need to know, from where I need to start so that the connection can be established from "what they know" to "what they need to know" so that students can grasp the concept and understand the subject.
3. Clear the core fundamentals & basics of that subject and explain how it is important, along with real time examples of where it is used, giving some hands-on practicals so that students can understand the concept and its connectivity.
4. Make eye contact to get the students' attention during the lecture so that they can pay complete attention to what i am saying. Ask questions in between so that students listen carefully.
5. At the start of the class, while explaining what we are studying today, explain the concepts with live examples and some activities if possible. Summarize the session. In the next lecture summarize the session again and start a new concept to make and keep the connection.
6. It's an art where we need them to realize how easy and enjoyable studies are with practical implementation and theory. Content knowledge should be strong. We should make the class interesting by not only reading out the book and explaining but also using different methods & changing the way of teaching Every time.

Dinesh: Do other professors also know these important things about teaching?

Poonam Mam: Yes, they know this but the way of teaching varies from one professor to another. It will come to us over a period of time and experience. She is a fresher so it will take some more time for her. I would suggest that you make **eye contact** whenever you are in contact with human beings in day to day activities. That will help you a lot. Did that answer your question?

Dinesh: Yes Ma'am, thank you so much. I understand very well and I will try my level best to make eye contact.

We both said bye to each other.

One Life Ends To Give Insights To Another Life

One day in class during break, we friends decided to bunk the lecture and go outside for a party the next day. We all gathered everything for the party and we were in the middle of the party when suddenly, one of our friends got a call from home, saying his brother had died by committing suicide. We all were shocked. We went to his house where the police and an ambulance were already there. They collected the body and went to the hospital with our friend. All of us went to the hospital via taxi to support him. We reached the hospital and called him. He said, "Come to the Postmortem ward on the 3rd floor of the building." We went to the 3rd floor. He came and hugged us and started crying. After some time, we all sat on chairs. It felt as if there was no air; I felt uncomfortable so I wandered around the floor. While I was walking on the floor, I suddenly felt cool air emanating from the other end of the floor. I went there and I saw there was a room whose door was open, from where the cool air was coming. When I looked inside the room, there were dead bodies all over the room. I looked at the room board. It read **"Post Mortem"** room. I was completely shocked and scared. When I looked inside, there was a Post Mortem table where doctors were doing the postmortem of a dead body. I stood on a side where the doctors couldn't see me and I just saw the doctors doing the postmortem. There was a strange feeling within me and my mind was blank for some time. I am thinking to myself, **"Every human being has to leave their body someday due to any cause at any age."**

While I was watching the post-mortem, the doctors spoke to each other briefly. One of the doctors said, "This is the body of a man who was a rich person when he was alive. He amassed all his money and property without using it and giving it to anyone. Maybe he thought he was going to take all of his money with him when he died. But he never understood the truth of life and he lost out on living life when he was alive." The other doctor said, "It reminds me of a story which my grandmother told me."

Visitors On This Planet Earth

There was a train going from "Mumbai to Delhi". The entire train was an AC train because of the long distance and it was a super-fast train. In the AC class, one person booked the ticket from "Mumbai Central to New Delhi". He boarded the train empty handed. A Railway Staff member saw the ticket and showed him his berth. He gave the man all the necessary things for the journey, such as bed sheets, pillow, newspapers, books, mobile charger, food, cutlery, liquid hand wash, etc. The man utilized the things one by one as and when it was necessary. He enjoyed the journey. It took almost 2 days. Now it was time for him to disembark from the train as his destination had almost arrived. He started packing all the necessary things that the train staff members gave to him. He started taking the bed sheets, pillow, newspapers, books, mobile charger, cutlery, and liquid hand wash. The staff member came and laughed at him. Then the man asked, "Why are you laughing at me?" The staff member said, "All of these things belong to the Railway & not to you. You can only utilize it while traveling in this train and you are not allowed to take anything with you. Please keep everything here. **As you came alone and empty handed while boarding the train, you have to go alone and empty handed while alighting from it."**

A train journey is the same as the journey of life. Everything that we get on this planet will remain here only & we can take nothing from here. Very few people understand this and live life by utilizing things, loving people with caring, helping and sharing. There are many people who think only about themselves and collect things without thinking about other beings. At the end of their life journey some realize it, while some don't and miss this beautiful opportunity of life which is no less than a gift to us to enjoy on this planet.

I saw the postmortem and heard the doctor's conversation, and realized it is true. Everyone on this planet has to leave empty handed one day, i.e., **"Empty hands when we are born and Empty hands when we die"**.

Some questions struck me: **"What is life if we are born and die empty?"** ; **"Why are we all living?"**; **"What is the truth about Birth and Death?"**; **"What is the difference between a body and a dead body?"** and some other questions.

Then I walked from there towards the place where my friend and all the others were sitting. I didn't say anything to them. All those questions were in my mind. That day, I wasn't able to sleep properly because of those questions & the incident.

The next day, my friend received the body and we all went to the graveyard. Over there my friend's relatives started all the rituals for the cremation. I went to a side and sat at one place. Seeing everything, I realized that this is the reality of life where I am running everyday towards this death. It seems like a dream but it is not a dream; it's the reality of life that everybody has to go through it one day or the other. After accepting this reality that **"one day I have to leave my body"** here, my mind was calm automatically and I felt peace within me for a moment. This is the **2nd incident** which happened to me and it made me realize the reality of life.

Discussion With School Professor

These were the things which I couldn't tell anyone. I was unable to concentrate on anything because of all these questions. After 2 weeks, one day I thought of going to meet my school professor to spend some time with him because he used to give some insights into his life and told me more about life. His name was **Laxmirajam**. I went to his house to meet him. We both met and started a discussion. He shared some insightful stories and then asked me something.

Laxmirajam Sir: Do you have anything to ask me or wish to say something which is bothering you?

Dinesh: No sir, nothing.

Laxmirajam Sir: I am able to judge from your face, that you have some questions. Don't hesitate; please ask so that you can get clarity about them.

Dinesh: Yes sir, I have questions. **What is life? And what is the truth about Birth and Death?**

The professor looked at me for some time and spoke.

Laxmirajam Sir: Listen carefully with complete awareness, focus and attention. Think of yourself as a third person who is listening to all these things. These are the questions related to the fundamentals of life. Very few people are this eager to know more about life like you. Other people also ask these questions but they are not as eager to know more about this and not ready to spend time with these questions. I want to know more about how you got these questions.

Dinesh: I told everything about the 1st & 2nd incident and asked again. What is the answer to my questions? Professor laughed at me and spoke.

Laxmirajam Sir: Well, I see you are very different from others. But to answer your questions, how can my answers solve your questions and satisfy you?

Dinesh: I did not understand; could you please explain more clearly?

Laxmirajam Sir: You have not got these questions from others. The questions are coming from you, right?

Dinesh: Yes.

Laxmirajam Sir: The answers also should come from you. Not from me. Even if I tell you the answers, your eagerness will still be there until the answers are coming from within you. My answers will give you some clarity. I suggest you work on yourself by spending some time.

Dinesh: I didn't understand. Could you please give some examples?

Laxmirajam Sir: Let's say you are in 5th standard but you get questions of the 10th standard level. Will you be able to answer them?

Dinesh: No.

Laxmirajam Sir: Let's say someone helped you to get those answers. Even then would you be able to understand the answers clearly?

Dinesh: No.

Laxmirajam Sir: Because getting an answer & understanding an answer are two different things.

Dinesh: What is the difference between Getting an answer & understanding an answer?

Laxmirajam Sir: You will get the answers from others who understand that problem & help in explaining to you what they know about it. But your questions and their questions arise from different perspectives and scenarios. If the reason behind questions is different, then others' solution will not help you &

your questions will still remain unanswered because the connectivity between both questions and answers is missing.

Dinesh: It feels like I'm understanding something but still it is not clear.

Laxmirajam Sir: Well, don't worry. Go home and set aside some free time to do one task.

1. Sit down in any of the comfortable positions you like.
2. Take a deep breath in slowly for 5 times.
3. Exhale a deep breath slowly for 5 times.
4. Refresh your memory to the point where we started our conversation. Listen to our conversation once again from a 3rd person perspective. To remind yourself again about our conversation, remember and see everything carefully about the 1st and the 2nd incidents along with our conversation.
5. Repeat this until you get clarity about why you asked questions and what answers are hidden in them. Make a note of each and every point.

I wanted you to do this task because everything is there inside your mind. This is the reason I wanted you to be aware from the start of our conversation. This task you can apply on a day-to-day basis to remember each and every thing.

Dinesh: Okay Sir, I will do this task till I get the answers from within me. I feel good and happy that I have a way to get answers to my questions.

We both said bye to each other.

Find The Person Who Is Aware And Ready For Death

I started doing that task everyday when I got free time and on some other days, I made time for it. After a week I got more clarity on life. Next day, I visited my friend's place for some work. The graveyard was on the way while going to his house. After the work was done, I was going back home but on the way, I observed a group of people near the graveyard, who were taking a dead body for cremation. I also went with them. I sat there on a chair in a corner and observed everything.

From that day onwards, I went to the graveyard and spent some time. I used to go inside the graveyard and sit in a chair, observing that people who came with a dead body, were talking about that person. Some spoke well and some spoke ill about that person. Some cried. I started going there as and when I got time. Sometimes people came with a dead body and sometimes they came for other rituals. Sometimes I sat alone and sometimes I wrote if anything came to my mind. It made me calm day by day. The caretakers of the graveyard observed that I was coming frequently; they asked me who I was, why I was coming here and what I was writing. I said, "I am staying at this location. I come here because I get peace here and I'm writing whatever comes to my mind about life." They said, "Okay." After a month, I observed that the dead bodies who were brought here had died because of these reasons : natural death, accidental death, suicide, health issues & homicide. I saw there were many people who used to plan each and every day based on their priorities. But most of them were not aware and not ready for death. I wanted to know if there was anyone who was aware and ready for death. If yes, then I wanted to know more about his life so that I could get to know more about life. I did not understand how to find that person. I did the task for a couple of days but still I didn't find anything.

One day, I was feeling hungry and luckily, I saw a roadside stall selling snacks for 10 rupees. I asked the vendor to give me some snacks. He gave me snacks wrapped inside the newspaper. I went to a nearby garden, ate the snacks and threw the newspaper in the dustbin. I saw the headline **"The man who died laughing at the Goodies 24th March 1975"**. When I saw the article, I was very happy that I had found exactly what I was looking for. In that article, it was mentioned, **"His wife wrote to the Goodies to thank them for making her husband's final moments so happy"**. I figured, **"If a person is ready for death and accepts it, then he will be happy and smile in his final moments irrespective of the cause of his death"**. I thought of doing a survey on it. I contacted the graveyard head and explained everything about the survey and why I wanted to do it. He agreed to it. We modified the form for the survey on death with one more point, providing the point 'Expression on Face' with check marks for 'Fearful', 'Scared', 'Shocked', 'Unknown' & 'Smiling & Happy'.

Whenever anyone came to the graveyard, they had to fill the form and submit it along with the regular process. After a week, I analyzed all the Death Forms but didn't find any single person with the checkmark 'Smiling & Happy'. I just thought, "So many people are dying. They are aware that everyone will die one day. Then **why are they not able to live life and smile in their final moments?**" When I visited the next week, I analyzed the Death Forms. In one form, **'Expression on Face'** was checkmarked with **'Smiling & Happy'**. I was shocked at first and felt happy. Then I asked for more details about that person. The graveyard head said, "We can't provide you with that." I requested them to help me, saying "I want to know more about life. Please help me. If the family members of the person are not ready to answer, then I will not force them or ask anything." He said, "Okay, but be careful because they already lost someone." I said OKAY.

I visited that address and went to that house. It was the 5th day from the date of death. I asked for the person named **Naveen**. They said, "Yes, this is his house. He is no more." I said, "I know that." They asked, "What do you want?" I said, "I want to speak to the person who filled and completed the formalities at the graveyard. It's very important." They agreed to it, asked me to sit, and offered something to eat. I was very happy and feeling hungry so I ate. Then a man came to me and said, "Yes, it was I who did the formalities. My name is **Swapnil** and I am Naveen's close friend. May I know who you are?" He asked me who I am. I said, "I am the person who is doing the survey. I need your help." I explained everything about the incidents and the survey.

Swapnil: It's good to see you as someone mature enough and eager to know more about life.

Dinesh: How would you know that I am eager to know more about life?

Swapnil: Boys of your age don't go to the graveyard in the first place and even if they do go there, they don't want to give much of their time to such things. But you go there daily as if it's a temple. Tell me what you are looking for.

Dinesh: You filled the form. The cause of death was 'Car Accident' & 'Expression on Face' was checkmarked with 'Smiling & Happy'. It was a car accident and he was smiling. How is that possible? A car accident happens suddenly, so how was he smiling?

Swapnil: We both were going to the market to purchase some goods from a nearby shop. We did not get one of the items at the shop so Naveen went to another shop which was at the corner of the opposite road. When he was crossing the road at an intersection, suddenly a car came and caused an accident. It happened all of a sudden in the blink of an eye. Then I called the ambulance & I held him in my arms. We both were looking at each other. He was very calm and there was no sound coming from his mouth. It was as if nothing had happened to him. The car driver came near us and he was in fear and shock. His body was shivering. He apologized and said, "I was a little drunk and suddenly at the turning, I was unable to control the brake and accelerator of the car." Then he cried and panicked. Naveen was in a position to talk and he spoke to the car driver.

Naveen: Don't worry, you are just intermediate to free me out of this body. Death is an important part of life which will come one day or the other. I have already been aware & ready for this moment for a long time because I have been preparing for my entire life since I was an adult. Listen, driver, next time onwards don't drink and drive, because it will destroy both of us and our families. You'll go to jail and your family will suffer. You are the one responsible for supporting and giving direction to your family. It's the same for me. In this situation, you are going to be there but my family is losing me. It is an irreplaceable place and it affects my family in many ways. The car driver cried and said, "I will never drink again. I promise."

Naveen: Listen, Swapnil, thank you my friend, for supporting me all this time and please do support my family as well in my absence. I am leaving & thank you for everything.

Swapnil: While Naveen was talking to me, he maintained eye contact till the last moment. When he said, "I am leaving & thank you for everything", I was able to feel the **happiness and calmness on his face, and the gratitude & love in his words and actions**, for everything that he got. At his last breath, he smiled. I was also shocked and had never seen anyone like him, who had a **smile on his face when he left the body or died.** That's all that happened.

Dinesh: You said, he was preparing for death his entire life. What does that mean? And how was he preparing?

Swapnil: I am also not sure what he was talking about and how he prepared himself for this.

Dinesh: Can you tell me about his hobbies, what he used to do most of the time & what he loved the most?

Swapnil: His hobbies were writing, painting and social service.

Dinesh: Can I get his writings & paintings please?

Swapnil: Sorry, we can't give you that. Those are his personal belongings & his family never agrees to give that.

Dinesh: Can I talk to his family please? Those writings & paintings are not normal things, the process that he followed & developed might be there in those writings and paintings that he gathered over a period of time **to enjoy death as a celebration**. Please allow me to speak to his family.

Swapnil: Only on 1 condition, that is, if they don't give then you will never come here again.

Dinesh: Agreed.

Swapnil took me to his family members. I was down on my knees and my neck touched the ground, then I told them everything about my survey and how those writings and paintings are crucial parts of it to help me to understand life because it will open the door to live life and it is not easy to enjoy death. I pleaded with them and insisted that I would not go until I got them. I looked at Swapnil. Swapnil discussed with his family members & asked them to give those things to me. So the family agreed & said, "Once you are done with your analysis please return back the originals and take one copy of those. That is the only memory that we have of our father." I agreed and smiled. I said, "Yes sure, I will return them as soon as I complete my analysis." They took my complete details and I thanked them. I asked Swapnil, "In case I need any help then I will reach out to you. Please cooperate with me because you are his close friend. Swapnil agreed and I thanked him again then left for the graveyard with those writings and paintings. I informed the Graveyard Head about everything that happened at Naveen's house. I left home with those writings and paintings.

I started going through those paintings first. Every painting had its own meaning about life and at the back, it had details about the message conveyed through those paintings. The paintings covered many things about each part of life with detailed insights and examples. Some paintings were very meaningful. I went through all the paintings. It took me almost a week to understand each and every painting. Then I started to read Naveen's writings from the start. It took me a month to complete that and understand every point by reading those writings again and again as he specified every point with a detailed example.

There were some stories which I would like to share, which clearly explained further about life and these are the foundation for understanding life.

Stories:

1st Story:
Truth of Life

This is the story of a conversation between an old woman and a woman in a hospital. The old woman tells the truth of life to the woman who will live only a few days.
Character Names: Suraj, Ashwini & Radha.
Suraj: I had gone to the hospital with my father due to viral fever. I was sitting in the chair with my father for a doctor's appointment. Suddenly, a paper fell down near me. I picked it and saw the names of a patient (Ashwini) and her guardian (Radha). A child came near me and said that the paper was theirs. I gave it to him. He went on to walk behind me, where I saw a woman on the stretcher. Maybe she was the patient (Ashwini) with two children (aged around 15 & 18), and an old woman who seemed to be her guardian (Radha) was sitting beside her stretcher. Doctor saw their reports and said it was final-stage cancer, so Ashwini had only a few days left to live. Then the conversation started between Ashwini and Radha. Ashwini started Crying and asked something to Radha.
Ashwini: Why this is happening to me? My children have no knowledge of life and the world yet. Their father is the only one who earns on a daily basis.
Radha: Life gives opportunities to everyone, but only few people find the time to know and experience the truth of life. Everyone's life journey is different and there are many ways to know the truth of life. I will tell you the truth of life which I am aware of. **Everyone is moving towards their grave** and very few people notice that we are not defined by this body and mind because of the principle, **"Empty hands when we are born and Empty hands when we die"**. Everything happening around us is only a dream.

The things that are happening around us are there in our mind and they do not reach us because we are not aware of our body and mind. We get information, knowledge and experience through our sense organs but they are outside the body so our mind and body always look outside. It flows according to the mind's instructions without our awareness. Once we spend time with ourselves and see within us with the help of sense organs then we will see, **"We all are divided in the united form"**. Because of that, whenever we help others unconditionally, we feel happy from within. Those who understand this, will spend some time with their self to understand about the self, the truth of life and death. Once they begin to understand the journey of life, then they love themselves and others who are around them, with happiness. **"Whatever is there inside us will come out"**. So the people who see the truth of life will be filled with love and happiness and it will come outside. There are some people who smile without any reason but you can look into their eyes to feel love and happiness.

We all come here to experience everything that happens around us including love and happiness. We have to accept and experience the things that we have and live life. We should know that all this is just a dream that will happen outside of us, and experience the truth.

If we know this truth, we can instruct our body and mind, and everything that is happening around us will not be able to reach us. We live in peace by knowing the truth i.e. every living being has to leave this body. Here, all these things are happening to help others to know the truth of life.

Everyone thinks that everything happening around us is the reality of life and we live life as it is. At the end everyone has to face death; at that time, they fear and die without experiencing the truth of life. Most of the time people live in the past or future. If they start to live in the present moment then they start seeing the reality of life with awakened eyes. Once we experience it then at the time of death (i.e. at the last moment of life), **"our body and mind will be calm and we shall close our eyes with a smile on our face by knowing the reality, truth & essence of life"**.

There are some people who are already experiencing it but are unable to explain it to other people who are around them. To explain the truth of life to someone is an art because everyone is in a different state of mind. The path they followed to experience the truth will not apply to others to follow the same path because the situations and conditions of one person are different from those of another person. So mentors will ask you to follow your own path to seek the truth and to spend some time with yourself to get to know more about yourself with the help of mind and body, by becoming aware of how both work. Once you are aware, then you start to live in the present moment.

Some people have already experienced the truth but are not able to prove to anyone what they are experiencing so they enjoy themselves and don't bother to explain to anyone.

I know you two children don't understand what I am saying right now, but listen to me carefully with complete focus and attention so that it will help you in future. **"Every single human being will never be with us forever in this world"** so we should be independent in all aspects to live life. It is the same truth that we have to understand and experience in life. Do every possible thing to live life in the present moment by being aware of each and every moment with complete awareness of body and mind. Once you are able to see the truth you will be filled with love and happiness because that is our default nature. There are people around us who are old in body but young in mind. They talk about love and happiness, but they don't experience it and don't know how to share it with others because they don't have it within them. They are controlled by their mind and they are chasing one desire after the other and they live in the past or future. Spend time with them so that you can share your love and happiness with them and try to awaken them if possible.

Uplift their mind by asking questions and showing the truth of life. Very few people understand and change, otherwise you must treat them like children with love and while talking, look into their eyes. Try to understand the emotional state of those around us. It is not their fault. It is not our fault. **What is inside us will come out**. Love comes when there is love inside. Happiness comes when there is happiness inside. Anger comes when there is anger inside. We must be happy with what we have and with those who are with us, without being overwhelmed by what we do not have.

Ashwini: Thank you Radha, for awakening me I will live the rest of my days happily with my family with complete love, and leave my body with a smile on my face.

Suraj: After listening to all these conversations, I thought about what she was saying, the truth of life which very few people are able to understand, experience and tell others. I started spending some time with myself then I learned many things about myself. Observe and understand people around us to see there are people who are old in body but young in mind, fear death, and are unable to live life with complete awareness and consciousness.

2nd Story:
Learn to live the present moment

This is the story of a person who helps others to conquer the mind. Explain to others with the help of a short story named **'Riding a horse'** which involves conquering a forest horse and riding it.

Character Names: Harish, Naresh, Grandfather & Mahesh.

Harish: Hello Naresh, I heard about you and I want to know more about living in the present moment.

Naresh: Can you tell me, Harish, how long you have been searching for it and why? Is there any reason behind it?

Harish: I have spent a lot of time with my grandfather, and he always says these things to me.

Grandfather: I have nothing to give you but I have something to tell you, so listen to me with complete focus and attention so that you can remember and recollect everything that I am saying. I have learned this over a period of time by spending some time with myself. I have observed, understood and experienced the journey of life. There are some fundamental things that you need be aware of:

Every human being has both body and mind. External organs of the body are visible to all but internal organs are visible through the scientific equipments. The mind is a fundamental part of the body which helps to process and work with other body parts. There are some fundamental things that are common to every human being, i.e., food, sleep, breath, self-protection & reproduction. There are **5 fundamentals of nature** which are the resources for many living species, i.e., **Earth, Water, Air, Fire & Space**. There are **3 important factors** which indicate **time for human beings, i.e., Past, Present and Future**. Most of the people live in the past or future. But to live and experience life, you have to learn to live the present moment. For that you can take help of the **5 sense organs, i.e., eyes (for seeing), nose (for smelling), ears** (for hearing), tongue (for tasting), and skin (for touching or feeling). These five sense organs help our body to interact with the external world with the help of other body parts. You can experience everything through these five senses, including the five natural elements. "There are two important things which will help you to live in the present moment at the initial level, i.e., eyes & breath".

Eye contact is a very important thing which helps you to live in the present moment. Make eye contact when you are talking to any person or seeing any animal. Everything that you do every moment, first you see it with your eyes for a few seconds and then do it. Eyes blink automatically on their own but I would request you to try to blink on your own for a moment.

Breath (or breathing) is an important process of human life which connects both mind and body. It will also happen naturally without any intervention. Try to draw your breath in and out, slowly and deeply on your own whenever possible.

When your body gets sick then don't get sick with it. Always see yourself as a third person and be aware of what your mind and body are doing. Calm your mind so that you can experience and hear the melody of the heartbeat. "There is no time to waste; you have to utilize your time wisely because every second counts. Everyone has limited time and you have to be present at each and every moment". That's it from my side. I am telling all these things to you because I know I can't take anything with me when I leave this body. That's it from my side, my dear grandson.

Harish: When my grandfather left his body, I could see the joy & the smile on his face, which everyone was talking about during his death. At that time I understood that he really experienced life because many people said they never saw anyone who died with a smile on their face. From that day onwards I tried to remember everything he said to me and searched on the internet to find details about "how to live the present moment".

Naresh: **I think you are ready; that's why you came to me** and now you are in a position to understand what I am saying. Listen carefully with complete focus and attention. **Your grandfather saw the truth of life, that's why he experienced life and accepted death with a smile.** If you see, everyone is moving towards death and they are running one after the other behind something which even they don't know. Everyone is afraid of death because they never spend time with themselves to understand death. I will tell you my understanding of death, which I get when I spend time on it. "**We all are guests here in this journey of life and everything that we find here belongs here only**" This includes all species, human beings, material things & non-material things, etc. Hence the principle, "Empty hands when we are born and empty hands when we die." **Death is our friend**, which is always with us like a shadow and comes anytime it wishes, to free us from this journey of life. But people who live here don't understand this and they try to live with limited people and limited things, and collect everything they want to take with them and miss the purpose of life. "**The purpose of life is to live life in the present moment with joy, happiness and love, with people around us, helping each other unconditionally without any expectation**". If you ask any person about an instance when they were happy, then most of the times they say they were happy when they helped someone without any expectation because "**We all are divided in the united form**" which means that our bodies make us different but we are connected eternally with each other through the five natural elements.

One more thing which I noticed is our body & mind, knowingly or unknowingly do **mistakes**. So, at that time **the involvement of our mind is 90% and that of our body is 10%**. But when **we punish ourselves for the same, our body gets 90% of the punishment and the mind gets 10% or less**. "**Our mind makes mistakes but we punish the whole body.**" Instead of that, we should resolve the problem at its origin by working on our mind which we can do by spending some time with it. In case you fix yourself only on the outside then the mind will make mistakes continuously because you have not fixed the problem from where it is arising i.e., the root level. I am saying everything to you because **knowledge is important but experience is what matters when it comes to understanding life.** I want you to do the '**Stop & See**' Exercise to experience life with me for a few moments. We will stand barefoot for 5 minutes. Here, the important point is that you should touch your feet completely to the ground for a while and observe the things around you, especially human beings, and tell me what you have observed. Based on that, I will tell you where you are in the process of living in the present moment.

Harish: After standing for 5 minutes, I have observed that everyone around me is going or running behind something. Most of the people are running but they don't have time to think about what they are doing because they never see with their eyes open. I think, in simple words, **"The mind controls humans."** but it should be **"Humans control the mind"**.

Naresh: I think you analyzed the essence of living in the present moment. The mind always tries to control human beings but it's important to spend some time with oneself to understand how our body and mind work & flows so that we can be aware of each and every moment. **We should instruct our mind and body to do things which are in our control.** Once we start this then we will conquer our mind and live life with joy, happiness & love by helping those who are around us. I must tell you, when I started to observe these things, I was able to explore the journey of life to the fullest.

I will tell you a story named **'Riding a horse'**, which helped me to conquer my mind.

One day I went to an animal zoo near my native place. I saw all the animals which were there in the Zoo. While roaming in the zoo, I went to a stable where all the horses were kept. Everyone was riding on a horse, so I went to a zookeeper who took care of the horses. His name was Mahesh. I asked him for the ride.

Mahesh: Please come here and climb onto the horse and sit quietly so that I can take you for a ride.

Naresh: After the ride, I asked him if any new horse was coming here and if yes, then whether a new person like me who wanted to ride on it could do it directly or there would be some process.

Mahesh: Animals roam freely in a forest and we bring them here, spend time with them and use them for a ride. If you are a new person and go directly to the new horse which came from the forest then it will not listen to you and it will try to run away from you; if you force it then it will hit you. First, you need to travel and spend some time with it so that you can understand the nature of the horse because the nature of every horse is different. You need to observe and analyze everyday, what it is doing from morning when it wakes up till night when it sleeps. You need to understand and see where it wants to go, why it wants to go there, what it gets from there, and what exactly it wants. You will observe the pattern and reason for doing this once you spend some time with it daily. Go near the horse and just keep quiet for some days so that it can feel comfortable with you. Once it is familiar with you then you can go nearby and it will not run from you. Then you have to do some service to it and touch it as much as possible. Try to give simple commands to it. For every 10 times you try to command it, the horse will listen to you once. Then it will listen to you after spending some time with you daily. Start giving small commands then it will listen to every command you give and later give bigger commands. After a lot of patience, one day you will conquer it and it will listen to everything that you say. Once you both spend some years with each other, the horse will automatically know what you want and it will do that.

Naresh: Thank you so much Mahesh. I understand your advice and I will get to know more when I spend time with the horse daily and learn by analyzing how I can conquer it.

We both said bye to each other.

I saw that our mind is like a horse that we are riding, but we don't know certain things about our mind like how it works, what it wants, why it does some things. It's similar to horse riding. So I started working on myself by spending some time with myself and being aware of how my body and mind works at each and every moment. Once I understood, I became a **"Human Aware of Mind"**. Still my mind always gives instructions to my body but I listen to both mind and body. I give instructions to my body by listening to my mind and thinking before reacting based on my observation, analysis, understanding, experience, knowledge and facts about life and things.

Harish: Thank you Naresh. I will definitely follow this daily and spend some time with myself to learn to live the present moment by being aware of each and every moment of my body and mind.

3rd Story:
Life is an Opportunity to Blossom

This is the story of a person who blossoms first and helps others to blossom by answering their questions.

Character Names: Prathamesh & Grandfather

Prathamesh: One day, I went to the garden for a walk. While I was walking, I observed a group of people sitting under a tree and listening to an old man sitting on a chair; they called him Grandfather. In front of Grandfather, there was a glass jar filled with papers. He picked up and read the pieces of paper one by one. In each piece of paper there was a question and its answer. Later, I came to know that the people who had questions, took the pen and paper from the organizer team, wrote their questions anonymously and put it in the empty jar. There were multiple jars kept at multiple locations around the garden. **Grandfather meditated on each question and wrote responses on the papers one by one, in the form of steps that were easy to follow and implement to make others' lives blossom one day.**

Next day I went to the garden for a walk. I was curious to join and get to know why so many people came there. I managed to get some time and sit down with a group of people to listen to the questions and answers. They gave me a pamphlet for instructions before joining the session. It said that the attendees of the session had to take actions on their existing problems to make progress in their life to blossom from where they were stuck. If they found any of the questions and answers matching with their problem then they would have to take action and implement the solution. If anyone delayed or failed to take action then they would have to pay the penalty of 50 Rupees every day even if they didn't attend that day's session. The money collected would be used to solve any of the locality problems which necessitated expenditure. I agreed to the terms.

Below are the questions and answers which I found useful to me & others to blossom their life by following the solutions given.

Question 1: What is life?
Answer: Life is a beautiful opportunity given to human beings to experience and blossom life. Experience every part of life and explore life to the fullest with love, happiness and joy.

Question 2: How to solve the problems or challenges that we encounter on a day-to-day basis?
Answer: Everyone's journey is different. The problems, challenges & situations people face on a day to day basis are different but the way they respond or react to this totally depends on their understanding of life developed by their own maturity and by observing the truth of life & others who are around them.

Question 3: What is the truth of life?
Answer: Everyone who has come here on this earth is a guest because we have to leave with empty hands one day. We are not this body and mind. Every human being has enough time and gets many opportunities daily to explore life to the fullest, both internally & externally; internally, by spending time with oneself, and externally, by spending time with people and things around us.

Question 4: How to live life?
Answer: It's every individual's choice and decision that they want to put in effort & time to explore and experience life based on their priorities, dreams, goals, ambitions and desires. They also keep in mind that they have to face the end results of whatever choices and decisions they make in their life. They have to live life each and every moment with complete consciousness and awareness of

both body and mind by learning how to live the present moment. It will make a difference in the experience of life on an individual level. It helps people to think before they act and react based on the circumstances that they are in.

Example: "**Life is 10% what happens to us and 90% of how we react to it**". Keep in mind that we have to love people and use things but many of them do the opposite. A wise man knows when to quit what he is doing, and to spend some time with other parts of life based on priorities and facts. Learn how much time we need to spend on people, things (Gadgets – mobile & Internet), priorities, dreams, goals, desires & self.

Question 5: What are the fundamental aspects of human life?
Answer: There are 5 fundamentals of nature which are the source for many living species, i.e., Earth, Water, Air, Fire & Space. There are 5 fundamental things that are common to every human being, i.e., food, sleep, breath, self-protection & reproduction. There are 3 important factors which indicate time for human beings, i.e., past, present and future. There are 5 fundamentals of sense organs i.e., eyes (for seeing), nose (for smelling), ears (for hearing), tongue (for tasting or talking), and skin (for touching or feeling).

Question 6: How to live in the present moment?
Answer: Every human being experiences life through both body and mind. Mind is a fundamental part of the body which helps to process and work on other body parts. Most of the people live either in the past or future. Because of this, they are not aware of the present moment and their reactions that they give to actions they get are not in their control. There are two important things which will help them to live the present moment at the initial level i.e., eyes & breath. Eye contact is a very important thing which will help them to live in the present moment. Make eye contact while talking to any person or any animal. Before doing anything see it

through eyes i.e. hold on for a second and then do it. Eyes blink automatically on their own; but try to blink for a moment on your own. In case you cannot do so, use your Breath or create your own way to live the present moment by spending some time with yourself. Breathing is an important process of human life which connects both mind and body. It happens naturally without any intervention. Try to breathe slowly and deeply on your own whenever possible or when situations are not in your control. Always see yourself as a third person and be aware of what your mind and body are doing. Try to give instructions to both mind and body. Calm your mind so that you can experience and hear the rhythm of the heartbeat. When your body gets sick, don't get sick with it. Knowingly or unknowingly if your body gets hurt physically then just keep quiet and observe that your body is hurt, but you aren't. Once you do this then you experience and start a new journey of life. This way you can experience life while you are alive.

Question 7: Is everything a part of life & make balance of it?
Answer: Everything that happens in this life is a part of life that makes you strong. Know the fact that whatever comes into your life will go one day. Every part of life, i.e., family, friends, work, learning, love, breakup, depression & loneliness, etc. all are only one part of life. Sometimes tough times come in any part of life to make you strong. So spend some time with yourself and accept it then concentrate on other parts of life because you shouldn't let one tough part affect your entire life. The past is not in your control but the present is in your control so make life worth living. Life is full of opportunities to blossom and there are many people who are dreaming of living life like you one day but you are already living that life; it's not a simple thing, if you understand. Always be happy, be grateful and enjoy the things that you have – both people and things, instead of running behind people or

things you don't have. Because most often people realize the value of something when they lose it. For some, there is a replacement but for others, there isn't. Always give your 100% love and happiness to people and things around you so that you can be happy when they leave or break. Try to maintain a balance in every part of life, i.e., personal life, family life, educational life, professional life & social life. Everyone has the same 24 hours but what makes a difference is how they utilize that time wisely in different parts of life to enjoy every part. Managing time & creating a balance in every part of life is not a one-day task; it's a journey which can be experienced over a period of time by spending time with oneself. "Most of the people learn from their own experience & failures. Some people learn from others' experiences & failures by observing and understanding". Many people already share their experience of this world in the form of art but very few people think, analyze and implement it in their own life. Arts can be there in any form, for example, books, quotes, stories, series, movies (morals, dialogues, songs), drawings, biographies, scriptures, history etc. "Observing one's own life from the day we remember things till the present also teaches us many things".

Question 8: What is the purpose of life?
Answer: The purpose of life is to live life. We live our life by spending time and collecting memories. The best gift we can give to others till they are with you is our time. Care for them like a child; make eye contact while you talk with complete attention, love and a smile on your face. Most importantly, whatever is inside of you will come outside so love yourself first by accepting and spending time with yourself by understanding the truth of life. Once you start working on understanding life then you will be ready to accept death with a smile on your face when it comes. The truth of happiness is that when we help each other without any

expectation, we feel happiness. We live life as though we are guests here then we give our 100% love, happiness and joy to others & leave peacefully with everything we have. Even when people leave temporarily or permanently, we say "**I gave my 100% love and it's the truth of life that whosoever comes will leave one day. The time that I spent with you and the memories that I collected over that period of time are enough for me to spend my entire life with love and happiness with those memories in my heart. Instead of crying over the people who are gone, let's spend time with those who are alive."**

Life is a beautiful gift given to human beings to experience and blossom so make it worth living. First you help yourself and then others who are in need without any expectation.

4th Story:
Deliver things to the right person in the right place at the right time

This is the story of college students & a farmer's child who work on their dreams from day one.

Character Names: Rajas, Sagar & Vinayak.

Rajas: One day, I visited my friend's place located in Kalyan City to combine studies for projects and interview preparation. We completed the combined studies as per our plans, schedules and timelines. We started preparing for the interview questions from the book which was suggested by our professor and he always said "**Every day is important. Taking actions towards your dreams is more important than waiting for the right moment without acting on it because when you act by using your time wisely, the right time will come.**" So we started when we were in the first year of graduation. We had gone through the important points that we needed to remember during the interview.

Now I was returning home to Dadar with the interview books and my laptop. I put my books in a different carrier bag and the laptop in my college bag. I reached Kalyan Railway station and waited for the arrival of the CST train which would halt at Dadar Railway station. The railway staff announced that the train was delayed and the rush at the station increased. The train was coming to the platform and I was ready with the carrier bag in my hands and wearing a college bag. The train arrived and I somehow managed to get into the train & rush inside. I put my bag of books on the shelf on the train due to the rush and held the college bag with the laptop in my hands. I got a seat to sit after some time. I kept my college bag on my lap. I saw that I had put my carrier bag on the opposite shelf. I started listening to music and after a while I saw that only 2 stations were left for the train to reach Dadar. I got a call from an old friend and I noticed only one station was left before Dadar. I got up and stood in the queue near the door. I was still talking to my friend on the phone when Dadar station arrived. I got down onto the platform and went towards the road to take a bus to go home. I waited for the bus at the bus stop. Suddenly I noticed something was missing. Then I remembered the carrier bag in which the interview books were there. I rushed to the same platform but the train had already left 20 minutes ago. I went to CST station via another train for which CST was the last station. I went to the enquiry room and informed them about all the details about my carrier bag. The railway official noted the train time, checked the train master book for the serial number and got to know that the train was on the way to Karjat and had already left from CST. I registered a complaint and returned home.

I was a part of the NSS Unit in my college. I was in class when we got a circular informing us about the 7-day NSS Campaign. It would be held in a school in Karjat. I recalled that I had heard this name before. Yes, I had lost my carrier bag of interview books in a train which was scheduled to go to Karjat. It had been 3 years since that incident happened.

We all friends prepared for the camp and we arrived at the school at Karjat in the afternoon. All the students received lunch from the school representatives and we heard the voices of people saying a prayer. It was all the village students who had started praying before eating. I observed that and asked a teacher in that school.

Teacher: Every day, we pray before eating lunch and dinner because we pray for all the people and animals who have contributed and worked to get this food into our plates. It's the gratitude from the bottom of our heart that we express in the form of a song, and we build a temple in the school premises.

Rajas: I got the essence of that prayer. In the evening there was a session, and in that session, our NSS Camp Officer introduced the Village Head Mr. Sagar and his son Mr. Vinayak. Our Officer requested Sagar to tell a story about the village and how the village built the school after so many struggles.

Sagar: Thank you Officer. It's my pleasure to share the story with you all.

The story starts like this: I went to the town to get some chemicals and fertilizers for farming. In the market I saw some people doing a drama performance on the road. Everyone was watching it so I decided to join the crowd to see what they were doing. So they acted in that show, conveying the message that if anyone wants to bring about progress in their village, then they must build schools and educate the children instead of promoting child labour. They shared a pamphlet in which was mentioned the thought, **"Education is the most powerful weapon to change the world and it's available everywhere around to learn"**. That day I decided that I would build a school in my village at any cost and I would start by educating my son. I started to send my son to the school in the town and asked him to do one thing, "Whatever lectures you attend in the school, you have to listen carefully with complete concentration and teach the same thing to our village children. Study very well in school and college so that you can get a good job and help our village to build a school." My son promised me and he started doing it but I saw that he was not taking the promise very seriously. I told him multiple times to take it seriously but he didn't listen to me. On Saturday I woke up in the morning but I was not feeling well because I had fever and body pain. I was not in a position to go for farming so I requested my son to go that day because it was important for the seeds otherwise the crops would not grow properly. On my request, my son went to the farm and came back. Later I asked him, "Is everything alright? How are you?"

Vinayak: I am fine and I understand how much you struggle every day for us to grow & get an education.

This one day of working on the farm made me learn the lesson that farming is not that easy to do as it requires a lot of effort, care and dedication to do everything to get the seeds to grow properly and get fruits out of them. I will fulfill your wish and I will build the school for our village at any cost.

Sagar: From that day onwards, Vinayak started working very hard with full dedication and he secured good grades in school and college. But he was facing challenges while giving interviews after completing college. He gave 10 Interviews but he was rejected every time in one of the rounds of interview. So he gave up on the interviews and started searching for other work so that he could utilize his time. I said, "Don't give up. You will get help somehow to crack the interview and get a job." He started preparing for it again but still he was not confident. One day I told him to go to the market in the town and bring some chemicals and fertilizers. He brought the chemicals and fertilizers along with a carrier bag in his hands and he was happy and had a smile on his face. He came to me, hugged me tightly and said that he would crack the interview and get a job in a good company. First I did not understand, then I asked what happened and what was in that bag.

Vinay: I went to the market and bought all the chemicals and fertilizers. While I was coming home via train. I had put the chemicals and fertilizers on the shelf and when I reach Karjat station I noticed that only a few people were left in the train coach and when I was taking the chemicals and fertilizers, I saw a carrier bag beside mine. I asked my fellow passengers about it and they said they didn't know. We reached Karjat station and I informed the railway police about it. They came with me to the train coach and opened the carrier bag where I saw that it contained books. There were no contact details in those books so they decided to keep it in the station storage room. I saw there were many things already kept in the station storage room, so I asked them how long these things had been kept here. They said that it had been years and no one came to take any of this. I requested them to let me take these books with me and if any one came for these books then I would return them. They agreed and took my contact details. I opened the books and I was shocked. It was study material to crack the interview.

Sagar: Vinay studied day and night. He practised everything that was there in those books and cracked the interview with a good package in a top company. He started saving money to build the school. After 2 years we started building the school and temple with the help of our village. We kept those books in that temple and we pray.

Rajas: Our NSS Camp Officer and students appraised both of them with plants. I was curious to know about those books so I went to Vinay and asked him. He said I could go to the temple and see those books. I went to the temple and saw those books. First I was shocked and later when I saw the name on that book I started crying with happiness in my heart. Later I kept the books and left from there. One of my friends asked, "I saw you while you were crying. What happened?" I said that these were those books which I lost 3 years back during our combined studies when we prepared for an interview by studying together.

That day, I learned a very important lesson about deciding to help others without any expectation. If a person finds any difficulty in fulfilling their aim, then they will get help to fulfill it.

5th Story:
Do what you love and love what you do

This is the story of college friends who met each other after 10 years.

Character Names: Suresh, Ramesh, Rajesh & Rajiv.

Suresh: Hi Ramesh & Rajesh, I have bought a new car and my company gave me a loan for it. I love the car. It's beautiful.

Ramesh: Hi Suresh. Oh great! My company does not give loans to its employees, otherwise I would have bought it. What about you Rajesh?

Rajesh: Hi Suresh & Ramesh. Right now I do not require a car so when it is absolutely required and necessary then I will buy it.

Suresh: For the past entire week I have been working on a project which has a deadline specified by the customer, and I don't get time to eat peacefully. My condition has been the worst during these working hours.

Ramesh: I am also facing similar conditions and my colleagues don't take work seriously. I have to spoon feed everything & it seems that they are not interested in working.

Rajesh: You both are not enjoying your work.

Suresh: No, I am not enjoying this work because I am not interested and am doing the same work daily. I'm just doing it for the sake of family because I'm getting a good salary.

Ramesh: No, I am also not enjoying the work but sometimes I feel excited and happy if any customer issue gets resolved because at that time, I learn new things.

Rajesh: Previously I was also very frustrated with my old job but I have switched to a new job. I love doing it because I am passionate about my work and each day, I feel excited to learn new things and improve my skills.

Suresh: Is the domain that you are currently working in the same as the previous one or have you switched to a different domain?

Rajesh: It is a different domain. You all know after our engineering course, I got placed in one of the top MNCs but I was not able to concentrate on my work. I felt like I was not interested in this work. Even though this MNC had good facilities like pickup and drop, games, good managers and colleagues, I was not satisfied with it, due to which I was able to use only 10% out of 100% of my potential at work. I managed to work 3 years somehow but later at some point in time I was frustrated and it was also affecting my family life. Every day I used to go to the office but I was unable to do my daily work properly. So I decided to change my domain of work. I noticed about my manager **Rajiv**. He was always happy and had a smile on his face at the office. He fulfilled his roles & responsibility very well. Everyone in the team enjoyed working with him. He guided and trained team members very well. One day he came to me and asked.

Rajiv: What happened? Is everything all right? Your performance was reduced in this quarter and I observed that on some days that you are not able concentrate on work properly. Please let me know in case of any issues and concentrate on work.

We both left for the day.

Next day, I went to his cabin and told him everything.

Rajesh: I want to switch my domain but don't know which domain I need to choose as I am not aware of anything apart from my current work and can't quit this job directly as my family is dependent on me.

Rajiv: I got your challenge and problem. What I can advise based on my experience is that you should spend some time with yourself, analyze your hobbies and check all the alternative domains which are available in the market and do some research on them. Obtain the details about whichever domain interests you and makes you feel excited. Go through all the study materials and tutorials, and look into the career paths in that domain from the beginner to the professional level. Try to get advice about that domain from the people who are already professionals in it. If that makes you happy then choose that domain. Try to go through the Job Description of the jobs available in that domain and prepare for it for a couple of months. If required then prepare for the certification in that domain so that it will give you a greater chance of being selected by an interviewer. Once you are capable enough for the interview, apply for the job in the respective domain then you switch the domain. I am telling you all this because I love my work and am passionate about it. It makes me really happy and excited every time. It makes it worth spending time on this work because it gives meaning to me by enabling me to help customers with my work. The most important thing I have learned about a job is "**Money can be earned in many ways. Do something that you love and find meaning in it so that you can be happy with what you are doing.**"

Rajesh: I thanked Rajiv for his advice. I spent some time with myself and I remembered everything that Rajiv had said to me. I started working on it and chose the domain "**Digital Marketing**" which made me happy while learning. After I went home, I started working on it for 4 months then I got an opportunity in that field but I failed at the start itself. Later I observed why I failed and started working on those skills that I needed to improve. Later I got an opportunity with a start-up. I discussed with my father & my family about my decision and told them that I was not happy with what I had been doing so I had decided on this new domain based on my manager's advice. The important thing was that I would get only 50% of my previous salary but I would be happy with it. For that my father & family said that they were happy with me, and not with my salary, so they told me to go ahead with the decision which made me happy.

Now it's been 7 Years since I started working in this domain. Every day I feel excited, learn new things, guide and mentor my team. Each and every day with this passion for my work, I love doing it with a lot of fun and enjoyment. Sometimes I get other work to do which I don't like but I have managed to do it with passion after I learned how to do work with passion.

One thing I observed about why most of the people are not happy with what they are doing is that this is because they don't have the knowledge of the domain in which they are working, such as where it came from, how it impacts the organization and consumers, how it is applied in daily life, what the Vision and mission of the organization is, etc. Once they learn everything about that domain for 3 to 4 months then they enjoy what they are doing. If they still don't enjoy it then they can switch to another domain.

It's every individual's choice to decide what they want and what they do. It's important to be happy with what we are doing. All we need to do is identify what we want and put in effort, time and money into it with complete focus, attention & patience. In short what I mean to say is **"Do what you love and love what you do"**.

All the friends got the important lesson from this story and said goodbye to each other.

These are all the stories which I heard from others or experienced written in Naveen's writings.

Dinesh: I understood many things about life from Naveen's stories and took a copy of all those writings and paintings. I handed over the originals to Swapnil. I experienced life by implementing those tasks one by one and analyzing those stories by spending some time with myself in different parts of life.

Waking Up All of A Sudden

I completed my 1st and 2nd year of graduation with good grades. In the 3rd year of graduation, the mid-year board exams were going on. I had received an external exam center near my location of residence as per the university rule. I prepared well for the exams. The first 2 exams went well. For the 3rd exam, I prepared well and reached the exam center. The exam started. I saw the question paper and marked all the questions which I could answer. I almost completed half of the paper. While I was writing an answer to one question, looking down into the paper, I suddenly lifted my head up and looked on all sides. A strange feeling came from within that questioned, **"Where am I?"** & **"What I am doing here?"**. It was like **"Waking up all of a sudden"**. Then I resumed writing my exam. After the exam, I remembered that moment in my memory. It was as if **"I had captured those strange feelings and moments"**. It was a very unique thing which I had never experienced before. This is the **3rd incident** which made me realize that there are certain experiences and incidents which give us totally different perspectives of life and new directions to see and live life. This incident was different because no one believed me when I told them about it, and I didn't get anything by sharing it with anyone. So I kept quiet and my inner self started to know more about life in every possible way. From that day onwards, the way I think about this life completely changed. Later, I completed all my mid-year and final year exams & secured good grades. After completing my final year, my college friends started to search for jobs. I also started and prepared for jobs. I gave 20 interviews but wasn't selected because I had not fulfilled their criteria in one of the rounds. I received feedback from my recruiters. They said, "You are a fresher and you are not fitting into our criteria." During the holidays, I woke up and stayed at home only. My father came to me and said, "What happened? Is everything alright?" I said, "No, father. I am unable to fit into the job criteria due to which I have not got any job but my friends have secured jobs."

Ask For Help and Support If Required, Without Any Ego

Father: Okay, don't worry. I would suggest you to go and talk to our neighbor Anand. He might help you. I want you to remember one thing. First you yourself understand what exactly the problem is and then work on it based on the problem. If you don't understand then discuss with others. **How would others know that you are in trouble and need help unless you discuss and talk with them?** This way at least you will utilize your time and contacts well. There are some times when you don't get help in the first attempt. You need to have patience and try with others. You will get directions one by one to solve your problem and get what you want.

Dinesh: I noted what my father said. I said to my father, "I have one question, father. Can I ask you?"

Father: Yes, sure.

Dinesh: How would you know that I am in trouble?

Father: It's simple. **I am your father.**

Dinesh: Tell me, Father. Please.

Father: I observed that every holiday you go and hang out with your friends but today you were at home and I saw your face. You looked upset and unhappy. So I thought you were in trouble.

Dinesh: Okay, I got it. Thanks Father. I will go and talk to Anand.

Getting Clarity on What To Do And What Not To Do

I was aware that my neighbor Anand was working in the IT (Information Technology) domain so I wanted to meet him and get advice from him as my father suggested. I went to his house and started talking to him.

Dinesh: Hello Anand. How are you?

Anand: Hello Dinesh, I am good. What about you?

Dinesh: I am good. I need some help, Anand. As you know, I have completed my final year of graduation. I am looking for a job. Do you have any advice, suggestions and references?

Anand: Yes, Dinesh. I am aware that you have completed the Final year of graduation. I have advice, suggestions and references as well. Before that, I just wanted to clear something so that you **get clarity on "what to do next and what not to do"**.

Are you planning for post-Graduation?

Dinesh: Right now, I am not but in future if it is required then I will definitely do either distance learning or a full-time course.

Anand: Have you decided the domain in which you want to make your career?

Dinesh: Yes, I have decided, I want to go for the IT domain because I enjoy tinkering with computers as per my academics and want to learn many things about it in future.

Anand: Okay, at least you have clarity on where to go. Do you have any idea of IT domains? Are you planning for any specific IT domain?

Dinesh: Yes. During my job preparation, I researched and found several IT domains: Software Development, System Administration, Network Administration, Hardware Engineering, Tech Support, Database Administration, Web Development, Cloud Computing, Project Management, Software Testing, etc. As I am a fresher, I am ready for any domain.

Anand: Okay, I will check and let you know. Do you have any idea about entrepreneurship?

Dinesh: Yes, it is an entrepreneur who observes and understands the problems faced by many people and tries to find the solution for it based on research. And provide a solution for it and in return he gets money based on the service he provides and he creates jobs for students and existing employees.

Anand: Are you looking for Entrepreneurship?

Dinesh: No, I am not looking for it because I don't have any knowledge about it.

Anand: Okay, if you are looking for it then you should have experience of that domain by working in that domain and understanding the process of IT of your domain and other domains, that is, how a company works and how it solves customers' problems and does business, how you will develop a business by understanding problems and providing solutions, etc. There are 4 business-based models in IT and everyone is adapting one of them, i.e., Product, Consultancy, Service and Solution Provider. That's all for Entrepreneurship.

Now for a job in IT Domain, I will suggest you to do some IT domain Certifications from online or offline platforms so that it will help you during the recruitment process. Share your resume with me so that I can forward it to my references. I will let you know about any references.

Dinesh: Sure, I will do that. Thank you Anand. After a week, I received a call from Anand and got a reference where they scheduled an interview. During the interview process, I said everything that I knew. If I didn't know something, I said, "Right now I am not aware of it but I am ready to learn." Then the recruiters said, "You are not fitting into our criteria." I thanked them and left. I informed Anand.

Anand: Don't worry, Dinesh. In any job, companies check whether the candidate fulfils the criteria for the respective job. If they see that the candidate suits that job then only they recruit him, otherwise they don't take that candidate. They have their own calculations so don't get upset. Let me check for other references. In the meanwhile, you prepare for the interviews.

Dinesh: After a week, again I received a call from Anand and got a reference where they scheduled an interview. During the interview process, I said everything that I knew. If I didn't know something then I said, "Right now I am not aware of it but I am ready to learn." I successfully completed the interview process and received an offer letter. I joined the company successfully. After I joined, I learned a lot of things about the IT domain and its services over a period of 2 years.

You Can Change Your Life; It's in Your Hands

One day, I was going to the washroom to freshen up. I saw a person crying. When I asked him what happened & why he was crying, he introduced himself as Yogesh and explained.

Yogesh: I came here for an interview and it's my 17th interview. Again, I was rejected because I am a fresher and I don't have any certification so I don't fit into their criteria. I am a middle-class person and during my college days nobody taught us that doing certification is important. Even if we want to do the certifications there are only a few genuine institutes who charge reasonable fees whereas the rest of the institutes just need money without providing good quality of education. There is no counseling provided in college or elsewhere to decide which course to do and what are the job options. See here, now I am struggling whereas the remaining college students who are aware or guided by their parents or mentors are getting placed. We struggle throughout our entire career to get a good standard of living. We work till the end of our life because of responsibilities and we forget to live our own life which we have got. That's why poor people get poorer and rich people get richer. Poor people get poorer because they don't know how to plan for financial freedom. Rich people get richer because they know how financial planning needs to be done to get freedom from financial problems. Poor and middle-class people are also human beings. They also want to live and enjoy life but they don't have any support system either from the government or from any source. All they have to do their entire life is work. This is what happened and that's why I am crying.

Dinesh: Oh yes, I can understand what you are going through all this time because I am also a middle-class person. Keep trying and most importantly learn from every experience that you are getting, whether they are your own experiences or those of your contacts, friends, neighbors, and mentors, or online or offline audios or videos (movies, web series or short videos or etc). Only very few people understand you, without you telling them anything but many times you have to ask them to get what you want by ignoring your ego, fear or overthinking of what they think about you or bad relations etc. One thing I can tell you for sure is that **"You can change your life, it's in your hands. All you have to do is think about what is more important and why and how you can add meaning to your life by observing yourself and surroundings."** Everything is at your fingertips via the Internet or offline so use it well to change your life by giving it time. If you don't give time to yourself then how can you change your life direction from where you are to where you want to be by taking small but appropriate actions. Not everything happens as per your planning or thinking or capability, sometimes **"you deserve better"** than what you are planning or thinking or capable of. Accept the change and move on, to change your life and inspire others by setting an example for them through the way you live life. One more thing which I want to share with you is that right now my age is 23 and it's my 2nd year in the company. There are some of my friends who were also looking for a job continuously for the first 3 years. Later, based on some other friend's suggestion they chose a different profession, i.e., that of an electrician, and they learned that skill. Now they are happy. There are some other domains which are good to pursue. Examples: Electrician, Repair & Maintenance of a particular product or all products, Agriculture, Fine Arts, Music, Massage Therapy, Teaching, Performing Arts, Fish Farming etc. All the best for the future.

Yogesh: I will do my level best to **"change my life first and inspire others"**. I will try in this domain but if it does not work then I will change the domain or create a new domain as per my interest. Thank you Dinesh for everything.

Dinesh: You are welcome.

We both left for the day.

I Wanted to Create A Platform For Those Who Don't Fit Into Criteria

This incident made me realize that there are many people who want to change their life but all they are missing is the **"Platform"** which will fulfill all their dreams by providing genuine and proper guidance without any expectations.

I completed 2 years in the same organization and as Anand suggested, I learned many things about my colleagues, IT and how the company works, and I did some Industry recommended certifications.

One day, I was going to the office by train as usual. All the passengers whose destination was "Andheri" got off from the train. While I was leaving the railway station, a boy suddenly started running back to the platform where we got off. I was worried seeing him so I also started to follow him. When I reached the platform, he started to worry more then he went to the station manager's office. I also followed him. He went inside the office. Then he came out and sat in the waiting area. I was watching him from a distance and I also informed my office team lead that I would come to the office in the 2nd half of the day because of some personal work. After around 50 minutes, the station manager staff came outside and called him. After 5 minutes, he came out, sat in the waiting area again and started crying. I watched him from a distance and then went near the waiting area. I saw a train was coming to the platform which was in front of the waiting area. The boy suddenly got up and started going near the platform. I guessed that his intentions were not good, as in, he was going to commit suicide. I went near him and stood behind him in such a way that he did not notice me. The train was coming very near to us. Then he crossed the red line which no one crosses as per the rule. It was confirmed that he was going to commit suicide. When the train was almost about to reach us, I suddenly touched his shoulder and when he turned back, I said, "The station manager's office staff is calling you." He suddenly started running towards the station manager's office and I went behind him to his office. When I went inside, he asked the station manager, "Did they get my bag which contains my certificates?" The station manager said, "Sorry, boy, no, I have not heard anything from them after our last update." I was behind the boy; he looked at me angrily and went outside. I went behind him and apologized for what I did. Then he said, "I am sorry." I asked him, "What happened? I have been watching you for the past 1 hour and I was also there with you in the same train and coach." For that, he said, "My name is **Imam**."

Imam: I have completed my graduation. It's been 6 months since I started searching for a job. In the initial stage when I went for interviews, they used to ask for all original certificates related to education, identity and others. So I always carried them with me for interviews. I always prepared for every interview by observing old performances. Today there was an interview scheduled at 10:00 am so I prepared well and brought all the original certificates. As this is the peak time for train travel, I kept my bag in the carrier or shelf as there was a crowd inside the train and there was a chance that my bag and documents would be crushed. When the destination station arrived, I was thinking about all the old interviews and planning for the upcoming interview. There was a crowd so I alighted from the train. While I was going to the railway station exit gate, I felt that I was missing something then I remembered that it was my bag. First, I ran to the platform but the train had already departed. Again, I went to the station manager's office and informed them everything. They said, "The train has already crossed 2 stations but we will inform the next station manager to check the coach." When they were informed about it, they said they didn't find any bag there. Now I am worried about my future and what will happen to me. Nowadays, everyone needs certificates and trusts documents. In society, all work is done based on certificates, right from the birth certificate to death certificate. What should I tell my parents? All the hardwork of this year was gone in just one minute. To get all the certificates, I need support and help which I don't have. For the past 6 months, I have tried many interviews but have not been selected so instead of burdening anyone, I thought the best way to free myself from this life is suicide but you saved me by tricking me. Why did you save me?

Dinesh: I can understand what you are going through because when I lost one of my certificates, it took me 3 months to get the original copy of that. I tricked you to save you. What you said is right. **"Everyone needs certificates and trust documents."** But you can live without them over a period of time as you are in society but later with patience, support and help you will get all the originals. If necessary, I will talk to your parents about it. I just want to know why you were rejected in all the interviews of the past 6 months. Did HR tell you any specific reason?

Imam: Yes, I had a gap of 1 year during my graduation due to backlog and I scored 55%. At some places, HR said that as per their policy they needed candidates who passed all semesters in the 1st attempt with at least 70%. In the other interviews, HR said, "We are accepting your grades but you have a gap year so you didn't fit into our criteria." Every company has different criteria which nobody taught us during our academics otherwise we would have taken care of it right from the start. One of my friends failed during the 2nd year of graduation due to some personal and family problems. Now he is struggling to get a good job.

Dinesh: Yes, I can understand it. As per my understanding, **"Every company puts forth their own criteria for candidates in order to filter the best candidates for their required designation in the company"**. This is how the industry works.

Imam: What will happen to those who do not fit into these criteria?

Dinesh: It's all depends on the person to person based on their situation, circumstances, family background and network connections they have to get job. If the person family is able to survive without his or her support then they get more time to search for good job which they like otherwise they will do any job on their way. Later it's their choice to continue the same domain or switch domain based on their situation and decision. Irrespective of job and its domain, very few people are happy, love and passionate about what they are doing, rest all doing the job for the sake of responsibility they have. As per my experience in this industry, out of 100%, only 20% of the people enjoy what they do. Others are just doing it for the sake of fulfilling the responsibilities they have or because they are okay with it as they don't want to complicate things. This is common for other industries or domains. Many people have hobbies and take breaks to balance their work life and personal life. There are some people who are not comfortable with what they are doing and then they make their own path by learning some skills which they like. Some people take time for themselves and analyze their interests and what they are capable of, then they learn that skill by putting in the required time and money with complete patience. The dissatisfaction or work pressure of the remaining 80% of the people will be seen in their actions when they are with family or friends or at other places. Everyone has their own choice of what they want. But most of the times people choose and think of what they want but do not take any actions then they realize that years passed but still there has been no change. **"Nothing will change until you do it"**. In the initial level of change, all you have to do is focus on the outcome and do something different daily as per your outcome. It is hard to accept the change and work on it. That's why people need to spend some time with themselves, and require support and help from their family and friends so that they can reach where they want. I hope you understand what I said. I will help you to get all those original copies again and talk to your family as well. One more thing which I learned over the period of time is that death is a part of life. It is very easy to die and it happens in just a few seconds. Life is a beautiful opportunity to give meaning to your existence, live and enjoy life while it also tests you a lot in every situation to make you strong enough to live and get an in-depth understanding of the reality of life so that you can celebrate each day, even in your final moments when you are dying. Make your life worth living by facing all the challenges and problems which make you strong day by day.

Imam: Thank you Dinesh for your kind words and I will definitely prepare myself for interviews till the time I receive my original copies. Then I will apply for interviews for 1 year and I will definitely spend time with myself, and take support and help from my family and friends, to get what I want from life and make my life worth living by giving meaning to it.

Dinesh: You are welcome, Imam.

Then we both went to the nearest tiffin center to eat some snacks. From there we both left for the day.

After resuming my office in the 2nd half, I left for the day. This incident made me realize that there are many people who want to get a good job where they can balance both work life and personal life. But many people are not satisfied with their work because they don't fit into the criteria which the company sets. In many cases, they are interested in and capable of different domains but their lack of skills and the domain criteria compel them to continue with what they are getting and they don't have any other options left. If they could get what they are really interested in and capable of, then they would reveal their true potential and put in their 100% which in turn would lead to an amazing outcome that no one would have ever imagined. It would totally be a next-level outcome. All they need is time, resources, counseling, training, support, mentor, desire and more importantly patience. The main reason why quality is reduced in every aspect of life is this.

There deep down, the voice within said to me, **"I want to create a platform for those who don't fit into criteria".**

About Social Entrepreneurship

After 1 week, over the weekend my friends and I went to the beach in the morning to spend some time. When we reached the beach, we sat and enjoyed the weather, sea and sky. While we were walking on the sand, we observed a couple who were cleaning the beach by collecting plastic and other unwanted things from the sand. They had already collected some garbage bags with plastic and unwanted things. My friends and I decided to lend them a hand. Once all the collection was done, they brought some snacks, and we all ate together. Later we asked them who they were and why they were cleaning the beach.

Couple: We are a couple and we got married last month. We were planning a honeymoon trip after our marriage. Our family and friends suggested different places. We finalized the location "Maldives". We both went shopping for our honeymoon. While we were shopping, we met our common old friend. His name is **Jagadish**.

Jagadish: Hi friends, how are you? Wish you a happy married life. Due to some work, I couldn't attend your marriage.

Couple: We are good, thank you Jagadish. Was that work more important than our marriage?

Jagadish: Actually, I tried to attend your marriage and also wanted to meet our friends but being a **'Social Entrepreneur'**, I have important work to do and the work couldn't be done without me so I was unable to attend your marriage.

Couple: You were a manager at one of the reputed companies, right? When did you change your job?

Jagadish: Yes, till last year I was a manager but I was not comfortable doing that job. As you are both aware, I have been planning my financial freedom right from our college days and after my marriage, my wife **Jyoti and I** both were earning.

Last year we both discussed our plans for the upcoming new year. I said to Jyoti, "I want to do something for society without any expectation. I took this decision because you are already earning more than me. We have a property which gets monthly rent and there are some other sources of passive income where we are not involved but I get my share of the income. You work for our survival and I work for society. **I want to live the rest of my life for myself.** Please agree, Jyoti."

Jyoti: I am always with you Jagadish. Do whatever you love to do. I will manage our livelihood and you will manage society. But what exactly are you planning to do?

Jagadish: I have studied and done some research on the term **"Social Entrepreneur"**.

A social entrepreneur is a person who pursues novel applications that have the potential to solve community-based problems. In short, he recognizes a social problem and uses entrepreneurial principles to organize, create, and manage a venture to make social change (a social venture). These individuals are willing to take on the risk and effort to create positive changes in society through their initiatives. Social entrepreneurs may believe that this practice is a way to connect you to your life's purpose, help others find theirs, and make a difference in the world (all while eking out a living).

In the initial stage, I will start with our home, building and society to understand the social problems. Based on that, I will start working on them. Later I will register the NGO and work under the NGO as a 'Social Entrepreneur'. The people who are interested will join us with the aim to help to solve community problems without any expectation. There are other Social Entrepreneurs; I will study them and if required I will meet them in person. One simple thought that came to my mind when I decided to become a 'Social Entrepreneur' is **"Nature and Society give us many things without asking. Now it's our turn to pay back those debts."**

Jyoti: It's good that you have gathered the required information. Let me know in case you require any help from me. **I will always be there for you no matter what the situation is.**

Jagadish: Thank you Jyoti, I know you mean that.
Later I started to understand all the social problems around me and tried to fix them one by one by coordinating with the required people. I respect those who responded and helped me during this process. On your marriage day, I had an appointment with one of the Social Entrepreneurs, which was scheduled 1 month ago. That's why I missed your marriage. By the way, what are you doing here?

Couple: We came here for shopping for our honeymoon and we finalized the location Maldives. In case you need any help during any of the activities or in terms of money, please let us know. We also want to pay our debt to nature and society.

Jagadish: Oh, that's great. Can I ask you something if you don't mind?

Couple: Yes, Sure.

Jagadish: Why are you going to Maldives & how much money does it cost?

Couple: We are going to Maldives **to spend some time with each other to understand each other better,** and we are planning to enjoy the sunset, watch dolphins and do scuba diving, snorkeling, jet skiing, skydiving, flyboarding, surfing, fishing & more. It will cost us around 1 lakh.

Jagadish: Oh, great. I have something to request you both to do as you are interested in paying your debt to nature and society. If anyone wants to do all those things at the beach they have to go to Maldives and they need to have 1 lakh in hand. What I wanted to say is that even we have a sea and a beach close by but we are missing the remaining things. If you are interested then instead of going to Maldives, you can spend that time and money at our sea and beach to make them better than before by providing the necessary things which are possible to provide. Later you can modify this as per your interest. Even you both can create new unique things at the beach, for which you both will be remembered. It will help our local people spend time at the sea and at the beach instead of going to other places like Maldives. I can take approval from the Government Municipal Department as an NGO to clean the sea, sand and beach. You can start with cleaning the beach by removing plastic and other unwanted materials. Later, you have to locate a place for all other things and we can take help of architects who are willing to help us for the good cause. This way, you both can come here anytime you wish without spending any money and it will also help attract other sea and nature lovers. **We can get some donations to amp up work on the things which we are planning for the future. We show the work to our donors and maintain transparency in our projects and donations.**

Couple: It is a good opportunity to repay our debts but give us some time; we will think about it and let you know once we finalize the decision.

Jagadish: This is only my request. Take your time for a decision. I shall accept any answer from you. You both are beach lovers so I suggested this kind of activity. People's choice of how they want to pay their debts to nature and society is based on their interests, creativity, requests, requirements, desires and needs.

Couple: We both thanked each other and left for the day.

We both discussed this and also informed this decision to our family and friends. They said, "We will respect your decision whatever it is." So we thought about it for a day and **finalized creating "Local Maldives" instead of going to Maldives**.

We informed Jagadish about this. He was very happy. We took necessary approvals from the Government and started working on weekends and whenever we got time. Our friends were also interested in joining us. We prepared and planned a year of activities so that we could share this with those who wanted to repay their debts to nature and society. We execute our activities as per the manpower support and funds we get. We share our progress with all those who supported us. It started 4 weeks ago, and we are getting a good response and support from people. Now we have observed people are coming very often to support us and enjoy the beach.

Dinesh: We thanked them for this beautiful opportunity to pay our debts to nature and society. We provided our contact details for further updates about their activities and the help that we could provide when we are free. We all left for the day.

Dream To Make a World Class Institute

Over the month, I also started researching about "Social Entrepreneur". I analyzed everything that needs to be done, what I promised to myself deep down and what the current challenges faced by society are. I planned and discussed with other people about how I could plan and execute things. Meanwhile, I got news from our college group that our college which was "Affiliated to University of Mumbai" had now become an "Autonomous unaided Research and Engineering Institute affiliated to University of Mumbai." I went to college as an Ex-student and asked the difference between the two to my favorite professor, Poonam Ma'am.

Poonam Mam: Previously, we were affiliated to the University of Mumbai and now too we are affiliated to the University of Mumbai but the difference is that previously, we had to follow the rules and regulations of the University of Mumbai and in case we wanted to change anything in our course, faculty, streams, etc then we had to request University of Mumbai. Once we got any approval only then could we apply it. But under the University of Mumbai there are many institutes so they take decisions and provide approvals by considering all affiliated colleges. This impacts the individual college performances because whenever they want to update anything, it remains pending due to delayed approvals from the University of Mumbai. So, our college board members, principle and staff members decided to make it an '**Autonomous College**' so that we can make our own decisions based on our requirements without waiting for anyone because we can now manage our own resources and funds. Previously we had to wait for resources and funds from the University. Even if we had those resources and funds, we could not implement anything unless we got approval from the University of Mumbai. We wanted to make this an '**Autonomous College**' because we wanted to make our institute a '**World Class Institute**' so that our country's students can get affordable education at our college instead of going abroad and spending lakhs of rupees for their higher studies. This way, we can set an example and open the possibility to other colleges in our country to become a World Class Institute if they so wish. This way, **the students and faculty will fulfill their dream of studying and teaching at a World Class Institute**. This way we can make our college a **'World Class Institute'** by updating things like courses, faculty, streams, infrastructure and placements, creating new records in this field, and raising the standard of education which will solve real life problems in all domains by making leaders, etc which are absolutely necessary in the current situation. We applied to become an 'Autonomous College' 2 years back and now the approval has been granted. I hope you understand the difference, right?

Dinesh: Yes, Ma'am. I have understood. Thank you for the clarification, ma'am.

Startup for Non-Criteria Students

I completed my 3rd year in the organization and now I was 25 years old. As I understood the IT process and became the Team Lead for Development & Digital Marketing, I learned the skill of Website Design & Development, Mobile App Development and Digital Marketing. I was limited to do certain things in my organization.

I personally helped my friends to develop their website for their business, with nominal fees for quality service. They said, "Why don't you make a **Startup** for **'Development and Digital Marketing'**? Nowadays development companies and startups are proposing more money for low quality service. If you propose nominal fees for good quality along with free Website Management Services for a year, it will bring in a reasonable amount. You can explore more and explore your own creativity in it. I said, "I will think about it and let you know."

When I discussed it with my family, Anand and my friends, they said, "Don't worry, we will support you from the perspective of money, customers and skills. I wanted to do something for **'non-Criteria Students'** so that they can get jobs and settle. I informed my company manager and HR about this decision. They said, "We don't want to lose you but it's your life and you have full rights to choose what you want. Let us know in case you need any help from us as you are an alumnus of this company." I said thanks for the support and help. After my notice period, I started my **startup** and placed all the non-criteria students as interns, which included both students and graduates who had completed their education. I provided everyone with the initial level of training which I purchased from an online platform for a 3-year subscription. The Online Platform had many tutorials about Website Design & Development, Mobile App Development and Digital Marketing.

There were also many additional tutorials for Cloud Computing, DevOps, Microservices, Database, Networking, Operating System, etc. I planned to create basic online tutorials and playlists for freshers to understand the concepts of IT so that their basics are clear. I knew one genuine Test Center where they could give online certifications with student discounts. Later I would train them in Website Design & Development, Mobile App Development and Digital Marketing. Then I would give them realtime scenarios and live case studies to create apps & websites. Once that was done, It was their choice to continue working with me or look for another job in MNC Companies, etc.

I applied all these things. It worked well for 6 months. I only received 10 projects during this time, that too from my friends' references but there were almost 50 well-prepared students, out of which 30 students left for MNC Companies and the remaining 20 were working with me. The 30 students also contributed by teaching other students, giving funds and sharing their skills & industry experiences with other students. This worked well and I was earning well because I was getting references from students who were learning here. Almost 11 months were completed, and I was recognized in my locality for the nominal fees, good quality and customer support for **'Development and Digital Marketing'**. Interns, students and courses increased.

One Works for One's Own Happiness and Another Works For Survival And Earning

I was part of Jagadish NGO for contribution to nature and society. I went to the beach on weekends to see the progress and many of my students were also part of it. We modified 'Local Maldives' well and we were getting a good response from the local people. We provided these things over a year's time of working with those couples. Local people and other tourists visited for Scuba Diving, Snorkeling, Enjoying the Sunset, Jet Skiing, Flyboarding, Surfing & Fishing with rules and regulations. Instead of asking them for tickets for each activity, we requested them to give donations as per their interest and enjoy anything they wished to, for any given duration of time. We observed there were some people who came daily, enjoyed and maintained those things by themselves.

One day, I was cleaning a Scuba Diving place when a lady came and said, "I want to make a donation." I said, "Yes, you are most welcome." So, she donated Rs.1000. As we posted the brochures for currently available services and upcoming plans, she took both brochures and said, "Thank you for this initiative." I said, "You are welcome." While I was enjoying the sunset, **she reminded me of Kanchana because when I saw her face and her smile, it made me joyful, happy and shocked at the same time**. This is what used to happen whenever I saw Kanchana. I left for the day. The next day, I went to the office and checked the status of all other projects. While I was working, one of my old students came to my cabin and said, "One of my neighbor's ladies wants to set up a website." I said, "Yes, please bring her in." He brought her in. At first, I was shocked and by the look she was also shocked. It was the same lady who reminded me of Kanchana. I said, "My name is Dinesh, please tell me." She said her name was **Lasya**.

Lasya: I have my own **beauty parlour** and I want a website for it.

Dinesh: Sure, we already have some other customers of beauty parlor websites. You can choose the design and services that you want in the site. The charges are nominal so you need not worry about the amount. Once the website is set up completely, you can pay the amount. By default, we will give free service for 1 year and later you can opt for services if required.

Lasya: Thank you Dinesh. I have one doubt. Yesterday it was you on the beach, right?

Dinesh: Yes, it was me.

Lasya: Okay, you do both the things.

Dinesh: Yes, **"That is for my own happiness. In short, I pay my debt to nature and society, and this is for survival and earning"**.

Lasya: I also heard you provide free training for non-criteria students.

Dinesh: Yes, if anyone wants to do something related to IT then I provide basic training with some online certifications so that they can get a good job in the corporate world. It doesn't mean that I train only students. All those people who are interested in learning basic IT concepts are welcome here to develop their skills. Some of my old students also teach in their locality and they come here for online certification.

Lasya: You are doing good work. But why are you providing training for free? You can at least charge nominal fees, right?

Dinesh: I am already earning for my survival through this website development and that is enough for me. I am paying my debt to nature and society in one way or other that makes me feel alive.

Lasya: Oh great, you are very unique. I will also try to pay my debt to nature and society in one form or other.

Dinesh: If you don't mind, I have one suggestion to pay your debt to nature and society.

Lasya: Please tell me the suggestion.

Dinesh: How much money and time have you spent learning this beautician course?

Lasya: It cost me Rs.1 lakh for a 2-year course.

Dinesh: Okay, you can create the **'Basic Beautician Course'** based on your experience and if required you can create or purchase some online courses to teach all the girls and boys in your locality who want to be beauticians, for free. You can take them for an internship and provide certification and training along with some live hands-on experience. This will help them and they can apply for jobs in other Beauty Parlours.

Lasya: Yes sure, I will make a Basic Beautician Course along with some online beautician courses. Let me know once the website is complete. Also, I will share the internship details with you once I have finalized them.

Dinesh: Sure, thank you.

After one month, the website was completed, and I informed Lasya about the website completion. She verified it and the functionality was as expected. When she tried to pay the amount, I said, "Please use that amount for the Basic Beautician Courses & training for all the future beauticians."

Lasya: Thank you Dinesh, for such kindness towards society.

We both left for the day.

Getting Clarity Through Discussion

Dinesh: One day I thought of going to meet my school professor Laxmirajam Sir again to spend some time with him because he gave me insights of his life and used to tell me more about life. I visited his house.

Laxmirajam Sir: Hello Dinesh, how are you? If you have come here, it means that there is a very important thing that is bothering you.

Dinesh: Hello Sir, I am good. Yes, as you expected, I have to ask you something which I have thought about for a while but I am not sure how I can do it.

Laxmirajam Sir: Tell me what exactly is bothering you. I will try my level best to help you.

Dinesh: Recently I heard about Autonomous colleges where they can do whatever they like to upgrade the college to become a World-Class Institute. I also wanted to do something like that but I'm not getting any clarity on what I need to do and how.

Laxmirajam Sir: I heard you have started a startup and are giving free training to students.

Dinesh: Yes Sir.

Laxmirajam Sir: Do you have any NGO?

Dinesh: No Sir, one of my friends, Jagadish who is a social entrepreneur, has an NGO which I am a part of and contribute to by doing some help on weekends when I am free.

Laxmirajam Sir: I know some of the Social Entrepreneurs. When I analyzed them, I found they had their own reasons to start their NGO or Trust and they worked for it day and night by taking small actions one by one as per their vision and mission. It did not happen all of a sudden. First, they saw the problem in reality by experiencing it or observing others and later figured out the solution for it. Then they analyzed how they could solve it and what resources they needed to achieve it. First, they discussed this with their family and friends to inform them and get their support because their family should have a source of income for survival otherwise it will be difficult to balance and manage things at both levels. They started to solve small locality problems first. Later, they expanded based on the requirements and resources they had in terms of manpower, monetary support, legal support and other resources. This is my analysis but everyone has their own ways of working.

There are a couple of things which I observed in social entrepreneurs or entrepreneurs. They wanted to do all the work by themselves. This happens due to a lack of confidence and trust in people. It is a common thing. But they cannot be present at 10 places and monitor the work at the same time. They should have trust and confidence in people, which comes through caring and helping. Sometimes people may not work the way you work or expected them to; at that time you have to analyze how that went wrong and how it can be corrected and learn a lesson from it. Be patient and teach them again. This is how you can achieve what you want to achieve on a large scale. One problem has many solutions and everyone has their own way of solving problems. Sometimes you have to trust them and give them the freedom to solve the problem in their own way instead of giving your own way. If it works then that is great, otherwise they learn a lesson and start working on problems independently on their own because you won't be there everytime they need help, right? We have a limited timespan to live life so make sure you give your 100%.

These are my suggestions for you. Now you spend some time with yourself and with these ideas. Think about where you want to start and at what scale you want to expand. Start your NGO or Trust at the local level with a single small room in a village or a city. Later you can expand at the state level, country level and global level.

Research the resources that are required to start it because there are many such NGOs already present across the globe. Even if yours duplicates others, you make it unique later. Resources might be anything like money, place, human support, local support, government support, technology support, etc. You can start helping needy people from now onwards by watching their actions. Help can be a word of help or a discussion to get them clarity, monetary help, caring, support, or any help which they need. But don't expect anything from them in return and never tell anyone about that help. Keep it a secret and forget about it because, "**Helping hands may forget whom they helped but the ones who were helped will never forget that helping hand.**" People should respect you from the bottom of their heart. You **start your journey because many things have become clear and you might get guidance during the journey** if you observe and listen carefully. I hope my analysis, observation and experience will give you clarity on what you need to do and how.

Dinesh: Yes Sir, your insights, knowledge and experience gave me some hope and clarity. I will research the rest and do the work.

I thanked Sir and left for the day.

Insights About Social Entrepreneurship

I started researching how I can implement what I want. I wanted to meet the social entrepreneurs directly in person and get their real-time insights, knowledge and experience. As I was already part of an NGO run by Jagadish, I contacted him and said that I wanted to meet him for some clarification. He said, "We can meet at "Local Maldives" tomorrow at 8:00 a.m. in the morning." I listed down what I wanted to ask and what my challenges were. We met in the morning.

Dinesh: Hi Jagadish, how are you?

Jagadish: Hi Dinesh, I am good. What about you? Yesterday you wanted to talk to me, right? Is it something urgent and important? Is everything alright?

Dinesh: Yes, I am good. I wanted to ask you something about social entrepreneurship and how I can implement what I want to implement. What is your observation and experience so far? Before you start, I want to tell you about a discussion that happened between my school professor Laxmirajam Sir & me. This is what happened.

Jagadish: What your professor said is true. Over a period of time, what I have observed and experienced is that there are many problems which need to be solved. To solve every problem we need resources like time, money, humans, technology, approvals from local bodies and government support. "**Understanding the root cause of any problem is more important than solving the problem**". Once the root cause is clear then only you can solve the exact problem otherwise the problem will occur again in the same form or a different form. The change that you want to bring into society, you should bring about in yourself first and later in the society because people say many things about it behind your back. Most importantly, anything you want to do on your own requires money, time and effort. No one will donate money to you until they are compassionate and know the value of what you are doing so don't expect anything from anyone. What exactly you are doing and at what scale will determine how much effort, time and money it needs. Plan accordingly, otherwise if you start to implement on a large scale and your estimation goes wrong, you'll end up leaving the work incomplete and no one will support you unless they are also connected with your mission and vision.

There are 2 things which I wanted to tell you about the city and the village.

In the city there are good people and bad people. Good people are those who don't hurt others and they are true to themselves, care, love and respect each other. Bad people are those who hurt others and always lie to save themselves and do anything that they get benefit from. The ones who trouble us in cities are bad business people who think only about their business and profit. They don't think about what they are doing, what the quality of service is, how it is impacting society and customers, how employees are treated, etc. They can go to any extent to run their business and get profit even if it kills animals and humans. They make problems in society and set up their business but if you solve those problems, they will be the first to inform you to stop those things. If you don't listen to them then they will go to any extent to save their business. One more thing: In cities the people live in a comfort zone and they don't want to get out of it but if you force them to get out of it then they will also go to any extent to save their comfort zone. Be careful.

As compared to cities, in the Village there are lesser people who stick to their old principles and castes. In some villages, people have a very good heart. They care for and respect every individual who comes into the village and lives there. If you find such a village then I will suggest you to coordinate with the village head and solve the social problems which they are facing. Later you give your proposal to implement what you wanted to implement in that village. Once you have implemented it successfully, everyone will come to you to take advantage of it, instead of you going to everyone and telling them about what you have implemented. The people who come to you will definitely understand the value of what you have implemented; that will be worth more.

Regarding implementation, it's all about your decisions and the requirements of what you wanted to implement in that village. This way you can transform that village into an **'Autonomous Village'** where everything is under your control and you customize it as you see fit. From there, remotely, through an online medium, you can interact all over the world, understand people's problems and provide solutions to them by understanding the root cause of those problems. All you have to do is guide them and once they implement the solutions then you can monitor them. **In such a manner, you can create this 'Autonomous Village' in a way that the world has never seen before, showing them that one village can control the entire world and solve all problems.** If you see and understand the depth of the root cause of the problems, then you'll analyze that 5 out of 10 villages face the same problem. This way you can create a solution once and use it in many places by understanding the root cause of the problem. This is all about my experience and knowledge about Social Entrepreneurship and Implementation.

Dinesh: Yes, I got your points. One more thing: Do I need to do any certification or degree for Social Entrepreneurship?

Jagadish: Let me tell you what I know. There are certain things you must be clear about before choosing Social Entrepreneurship, that is, whether you want to **'work in silence' or 'want to show'**. Let me clarify both these things.

'**Work in silence**' means you solve the problem and keep quiet; you do not tell everyone unnecessarily until and unless it is important. '**Want to show**' means you solve the problem and tell everyone without their asking. Once this is clear then you can decide which one you prefer but I suggest you to choose "Work in silence". This way you can concentrate on things which are important.

For Social Entrepreneurship, previously there were no certifications or degrees but nowadays some universities, NGOs, online platforms or corporates provide both online and offline courses or workshops for it. Some are free and some take nominal fees. Based on your requirement you choose which one suits you. I would prefer that you study online for free and **take an ID card** from that particular NGO or University or Corporate, which serves as proof that you are a Social Entrepreneur. It is required when you are doing any work in society or requesting funds for any activity because no one listens to you if you speak by yourself; you need to show your ID card and say, "What I did is that **I created my own NGO and have an ID card of a 'Social Entrepreneur'.**" If you don't want to create an NGO, you can be part of any NGO and give a written justification about why you need a 'Social Entrepreneur' ID card. Take complete responsibility for what you are doing and submit everything that you are doing. This way you can track what you are doing and it will help you to get resources. There are certain things which you can do alone and for other things you need a team. For the team, don't ask anyone to join you because they don't know about your vision and mission and they don't enjoy what they are doing. In short, **they don't realize the value of it**. Let the people come and join you. This way they will take initiative and do the work without telling you, and by realizing the value of it, they enjoy as well. If someone leaves your team, respect their decision and thank them for their contribution. I hope you got the answer which you are looking for.

Dinesh: Yes, Jagadish, thank you so much.

We both left for the day.

I started researching all over the world about the problems and solutions that are already implemented and which I can implement in the 'Autonomous Village'. One thing had become clear to me during this discussion. I needed to work on my communication skills, increase my network of contacts and be financially independent so that I could implement what is necessary without thinking about the cost.

One day, when I was spending time with my family, my dad said, "Now your age is 26. It's the perfect age for marriage in our society so we are looking for matches for your marriage. Do you know or love anyone already? Let us know before it's too late." I said, "Give me a month. I will decide and tell you." On weekdays, I worked on my projects and trained students. On the weekend, I went to the beach, i.e., 'Local Maldives' to spend time with myself. When I visited the place, I saw Lasya helping children in some activities. She saw me and greeted me.

Lasya: Hi Dinesh, good morning. How are you?

Dinesh: Hi Lasya, good morning. I am good. What about you?

Lasya: I am good. Is everything alright? Is anything bothering you?

Dinesh: Everything is alright. I'm just thinking about my dream.

I told her everything about the 'Autonomous Village' and I asked how her Beauty Parlour and Beautician Course was going.

Lasya: You have a very unique dream and I am proud of you. Please let me know if you need any help from my side. As for me, both, the beauty parlour and the course are going well.

Dinesh: I wanted to tell you something which is personal and it's bothering me. Before that I want to ask whether you are single or in a relationship.

Lasya: Yes, dinesh. Tell me, how can I help you? I am single.

Dinesh: I said everything about Kanchana, and how I was shocked and felt connected when I saw her, the same way that I felt when I saw Kanchana. Now my parents are looking for a match for marriage. I asked them for 1 month. I wanted to spend this 1 month with you so that we can get to know each other and at the end we can decide whether we can live with each other for the rest of our life or only be good friends forever. Let me know your decision to spend this one month with me.

Lasya: Anyway my parents are looking for matches. I will spend one month with you. Later, we will decide.

Dinesh: We spent 1 month getting to know each other. We discussed these points in detail from both points of view: Understanding, trust, respect, caring, responsibility, patience, support, wealth management, attraction to each other. We agreed to certain terms and conditions. We also decided on a funny penalty if we cross those terms and conditions. We had heard about the 'Forget and Forgive' principle from our friends. First we apply the 'Forget and Forgive' principle to connect with each other with proper communication. At the end of the month, we decided to live with each other for the rest of our lives. We also conveyed the same decision to our parents. First they disagreed because we belong to different castes. After 6 months of trying they agreed because they love us. We both got married.

After marriage, our parents suggested we go somewhere on our honeymoon to spend time with each other. For that, we both said, "We have already planned where we want to go and what we want to do. In our locality there is a huge garden but there is no maintenance from the local bodies. We have decided to renovate that garden with our honeymoon cost. In that garden we will plant all kinds of beautiful and rare flowers along with some exercise equipment for kids and adults so that people can come and experience it here and spend some time with their family and with nature." For that our parents agreed and they also helped us to renovate it with both old and new techniques.

I decided to concentrate on my startup first so that I could be independent financially and help people around me in the office and other surroundings on a small scale instead of focusing on major social problems. My wife was also doing the same thing. Until we were financially independent, we decided to research all over the world about what we could do in that Autonomous Village.

Set An Example For Others Through The Way You Live

After 21 years of hard work on the startup, I managed to open one branch overseas (in a foreign country) because many of my clients belonged to that place. One day, one of my clients invited me to a meeting to propose my services. I proposed all my business strategies in the meeting & it was successful. I received good responses from the new customers.

While I was touring that place, I saw a person with a smile on his face, sitting in a garden chair. The next day, I again saw that person with a smile on his face. I was able to remember that I had seen him somewhere but I had visited that place for the first time. At that time, I was totally confused, not understanding where I had seen him. I decided to talk to him to get some clarity. I went near him and sat in the chair next to his. He looked at me and smiled. I also smiled at him and introduced myself. He also introduced himself saying, "My name is **Martin**."

Dinesh: Hi Martin, I have something to ask you. Can I ask you?

Martin: Yes, please go ahead.

Dinesh: I've seen you somewhere but I am unable to recollect where I saw you.

Martin: Yes, I remember you. We met at the Conference for Managing Financial Planning for Industries.

Dinesh: Yes, I remember now. You were a top industrialist at that time. It was about 5 years ago.

Martin: Yes, that was my last conference. Later I resigned as CEO and now I am only a former advisor for that company.

Dinesh: Oh, but why did you resign? Just curious to know because you are in your 40's and not even of the age to retire.

Martin: Yes, I was 42 years old at that time. I also wanted to be CEO till I reached the official retirement age but one incident changed my life totally.

Dinesh: Could you please share with me the incident that made you take such a decision?

Martin: Yeah sure, it's my pleasure to share this with you. Before that let me tell you some of my observations.

In today's world, there are many people who have inherited their parents' & grandparents' money in the form of business or property or in many other ways. Some people get rich through a unique art or skill or knowledge or expertise in something that solves a problem or has demand for getting things done, and in return they get money.

I call people rich by money if they have money where their children and grandchildren live without doing any work. Most of the time, that person's worries are all about how he manages that money or how his children & grandchildren handle that money. Sometimes handling money also makes you lose your peace.

Now I have questions for you about how you manage your money.

Dinesh: I also observed this in India that people who are rich by money lose their peace while managing that money. Regarding your question, for me, it's very challenging to manage money. I have my financial planning to manage all of it but still it is a very tedious task to manage that much money.

Martin: Have you donated your money anywhere?

Dinesh: Yes, sometimes when I feel like **"spending is more important than saving"**.

Martin: Okay, I wanted to ask you something more before I tell you about my incident because you might also transform your life. Is your dad alive?

Dinesh: No, he died 5 years ago due to health issues.

Martin: You are rich but I just want to know whether you became rich through your own hardwork or this is your dad's business.

Dinesh: It is my hard work; my dad was a middle-class person.

Martin: Do you ever worry about how your children will use or manage your money if anything suddenly happens to you?

Dinesh: I have planned and set aside some money for their future so that they can settle. After they settle, I'm not sure how they will manage this money & I was worried that they would be unable to do so.

Martin: I think I can start sharing my incident.

I have a hobby of swimming. I usually go to different cities for swimming. One day I met **Joseph** while swimming. Later, I came to know that he was also a billionaire. We usually discussed our respective companies' growth, our personal growth, weekend trips & plans and solutions for any problem that we were facing. We became close friends and 6 months passed. We usually travelled as and when we got time. Suddenly one day I got a call from him saying he needed to talk to me & he gave me a hospital's address. I was a bit worried. I visited the hospital as soon as possible and met Joseph.

Martin: Hi Joseph, how are you? What happened to you?

Joseph: I am good now but I had a cardiac arrest. I was doing some office work but suddenly my chest started to hurt. I called my wife and she arranged everything. Now I am feeling good. There is a reason why I called you. I need a favour from you. This is my son **Michael**. You need to support him in my business in case anything happens to me.

Martin: Sure, I will take care of him and support him in every possible way.

Joseph: Michael, you go outside, I need to talk to Martin in private. Martin, listen carefully. These are my private accounts and the ownership has already been transferred to you. I want you to use it wisely whenever you feel necessary.

Martin: But why are you giving it to me now? Give it to your family.

Joseph: My family already has enough money to live without worries, doing my business & their own work. The important thing that happened when I got the cardiac arrest was that I saw all my family members in front of me & I was worried about my private money and property. As in, I am unable to use it well. All I did was keep it in bank accounts. The most important thing about the reality of life came into my mind when I got cardiac arrest. **"People born & die empty handed."** I previously knew this as a thought, but that day when I suddenly collapsed, I really experienced it and felt that I was taking nothing with me. The only thing I remembered was the time **I helped a stranger by sharing my food while travelling**. That feeling of having helped someone without any expectation was amazing. Earlier I didn't have the courage to give my money to anyone freely without any expectations. But now, I see I couldn't take a single penny when I was about to die. All my money will be in private accounts & later it will go to my nominees. Some money without any nominees will be unnoticed and it will be there without any use. All over the world, there are many people who are working day & night all their life for this money. They didn't even live their life for themselves; everyone has their own responsibility which they have to fulfill as per the needs of their family and society. Now I have the opportunity to spend my money through you.

I just thought that if any of my maids or workers or employees were to get a cardiac arrest & they died due to lack of resources, then their family would have to suffer & most of them don't have any idea about financial planning and they think, **"What happens to my family if I die?"** This is because all they earn will be over by month-end and they don't have enough money for their savings for the future even if they want to save. I want to spend some money for them because they worked for me all their life & now, I think it's my turn to make them financially secure as much as possible. "**I am not doing this for free; I am in debt to them for** their trust and loyalty towards me for all these years". I want you to go and get all their family members health insurance, and term insurance for salaried persons so that they ensure that their family has some financial freedom in their absence. All the insurance policies will need to be easy for them instead of their family running behind policy claims for follow ups. The rest of the money, you spend wherever you wish, as you see fit and as required. Please do me this favour because I'm not sure how much time I have left to live.

Martin: Don't worry, nothing will happen to you. I will do as you said & I will get both Health and Term insurances for your maids, workers & employees too. I will also do it for my maids, workers & employees too. I will also make sure all the people get genuine services from insurance service providers so that they don't have to struggle for money if they get unhealthy otherwise their family members will be troubled by claim settlement follow ups.

Joseph: Thanks Martin. Now I am feeling happy that all my hard-earned money is spent for a good cause instead of being kept in banks without any use.

Martin: After 1 week, Joseph died and I received the recording of 1 week's footage from Michael. In that recording, there was a message. "It was my dad's last request to put a CCTV camera in the bedroom and all the places he goes to. He said, 'In case I die, send that footage to Martin.'"

I wondered why anybody would send their death footage to me. There might be something he wanted to say through that footage. Let's look at it very carefully. After seeing the footage for the first time, I noticed that for 1 week he was very happy. He treated all his family members, maids and workers very happily with respect and love and they also happily treated him with respect and love. Later I thought I was missing something so I saw the footage around 5 times from start to end. I understood what Joseph wanted to tell me. That incident changed me & now I am here sitting peacefully & happily without any worries about my money, children & business.

Dinesh: That gave me some really great insight about spending all the money that we have earned over a period of time for a good cause. I am curious to know what Joseph wanted to tell you & what you got from that footage.

Martin: I will not be able to tell you in words what I saw but I can share the recordings with you for you to see it yourself. I think I want you to notice his face at the time of death. Now I have some work. Please give me a call-in case you need my help.

Dinesh: Sure, share the recording with me.

After watching the recording, a couple of times, I noticed the happiness on Joseph's face and the love in his actions for that 1 week. I saw **that Joseph was smiling while he was dying.**

I returned back to India.

This incident reminded me of **Naveen** who died in an accident but with a smile and a happy expression on his face. I again went through those writings & paintings. Now this time, it took me a month to do so, but it gave me different insights.

Research and Report on Lack of Treatment And Issue Of Affordability

After that incident with Martin, I recollected all my memories from the day I met Martin till I returned to India. Joseph's story really gave me insight about how a family member's health insurance and a salaried person's term insurance will help and support that family financially. Most of the low- and middle-class people die from lack of treatment because the treatment in private multispecialty hospitals is not affordable.

At night, when I tried to sleep, I kept remembering this statement again and again:

"I am not doing this for free; I am in debt to them for their trust and loyalty towards me for all these years". I want you to go and get all their family members health insurance, and term insurance for salaried persons so that they can ensure that their family will have some financial freedom in their absence.

Next day, I went to my research team in the office and shared the incident with them. I asked them to do research on the topics 'lack of treatment' and 'lack of affordability', and provide complete information about it.

They said, "We will share the report as soon as we get all the required and complete information."

After 1 week, I received a detailed report on it.

Report Starts:

There are 8.6 million deaths every year in low and middle-income countries (134 countries) — the majority of the world— that could have been saved with good-quality health systems. These were deaths from treatable conditions because people didn't get good care.

Of those 8.6 million, the study estimates that 5 million people die every year because of poor-quality health care in low and middle-income countries. These are the people who got treatment but of poor quality. The remaining 3.6 million people in those countries die from not having access to care, which has been the traditional focus in global health.

Poor quality care leads to more deaths than insufficient access to healthcare —1.6 million Indians died due to poor quality of care in 2016, nearly twice as many as those who died due to non-utilisation of healthcare services (838,000 persons).

Public accountability and transparency in the health system functioning are two ways to improve the quality of healthcare, the commission recommends.

A third of patients (34%) in low and middle-income countries report poor user experience, citing lack of respect, long waiting periods and short consultations, the report says.

"Initial and continuing professional education of health care providers must emphasize care, concern, compassion, courtesy and respectful communication as essential elements of health service provision, whether it is individual patients they are dealing with in clinical care or communities in public health".

"For this to be actualized, we need technical and financial audits to be supplemented by social audits measuring people's levels of satisfaction with and utilization of health services".

One must concentrate on 'Cost of poor-quality care', 'Equal importance of quality and access', 'Poor user experience' and 'The right to high quality care'.

To improve the healthcare system, we identified four universal actions:

The first is establishing a system-wide focus on quality, because there's no accountability today. There's no system to sound an alarm, and there needs to be one.

Second, you've got to redesign health systems. A lot of health systems today are organized to maximize access — a lot of small clinics spread out over a large territory.

Third, the health workforce education in many low and middle-income countries is just really outdated. Clinicians come out very good at identifying pathologies on slides but have a harder time doing problem-solving and connecting with patients.

And then the last area of improvement for us is public demand. In most service industries, it is the pressure of customers that often improves the product or service. Yet in health care, we ignore patients as consumers. Many people anticipate low quality and have low expectations. But people do want good care.

Report Ends.

About My NGO, My Company & My Family

I have learned many things about life. On weekends, I visit all over the world to know more about the world, how people live and the common challenges they face. I wanted to be in a position to change things around me. For that, I decided to make myself financially independent so that I could help those in need, change things around me and use money wherever needed to improve. Once I analyzed everything, I started an NGO with the help of my family and friends so that it could be used as a medium to contact needy people. Some came to me via the NGO for seeking help and sometimes I went to those people via the NGO. I ran this for 5 years but later because of Business competition, I was unable to give much time & focus on the NGO but in my absence my friends started to manage and run it.

It's been 22 years since I founded my Startup and now my age is 47. I have gone through many challenges and faced many competitions as the CEO of my company. My company is also recognized as a **"Great Place to Work"** in MNC's. I have created a software which will help all customers to customize their website based on plugins. Now it's a Product and Consultancy based company providing Consultancy in IT to other industries.

Regarding my family life, you already know about my marriage and my wife **"Lasya"**. I have 2 children, a girl named **Amrutha** and a boy named **Akash**. I asked my children to spend some time by themselves and let me know what they want to become in life. I asked them to do what they love. I told them, "It's your life & you should take complete responsibility for it in every situation & have confidence in yourself. Take your own time to decide what you want to be by spending some time alone by yourself."

I have given them complete freedom to choose their career.

My daughter said she wanted to learn Business. I have involved my daughter in this business for 5 years as a Trainee to improve the company's products and achieve its vision & mission so that she can learn everything about business.

My son said he wanted to go into the domain of music as he is passionate about music and playing various instruments. I said, "Do what you love to do."

I have given my support, help and attention whenever they needed it on priority.

Decision On Health Insurance and Term Insurance

When I analyzed the report, I found they had not specified how many families suffer as a result of losing a salaried person or family member due to lack of treatment and resources. Even if they want to get good treatment, it is only available in the private multispecialty hospitals which they cannot afford.

When I discussed this issue with my research team, HR team & friends, I found that as an organization we only took health insurance of employees, their husband/spouse and their 2 children for a period of 1 year, and renewed it each year till the time the employee was still working in the company.

When I discussed this with Insurance companies for a solution based on my requirements, they said the policy would be applicable to whole family, inclusive of all services with complete support and guidance.

Health Insurance - Covered: Whole Family, Time: Lifetime, Sum Assured: 5 Cr, Premium: 10 lakhs.

Term Insurance - Covered: Whole Family, Time: Lifetime, Sum Assured: 2 Cr/person, Premium: 10 lakhs.

I applied this in my company and made it compulsory for every employee. All the premium would be paid by the company, for existing employees as soon as possible, and for new employees, at the time of joining. If anyone left the organization then also this insurance would still apply.

If an employee died due to any reason then their family members would get half of the salary. The company would bear the cost of the education of their children, who would also be provided a job in the company or training to get a job in other companies as per their wish.

The NGO would be used for all the employees who have maids, drivers, workers, daily wage earners and other people who also took this insurance at the rate of Rs.100 per family per month, and remaining amount would be paid by the NGO.

Health Insurance - Covered: Whole Family, Time: Lifetime, Sum Assured: 3 Cr, Premium: 5 lakhs.

Term Insurance - Covered: Whole Family, Time: Lifetime, Sum Assured: 1 Cr/person, Premium: 5 lakhs.

If anyone's Health Insurance was utilized fully then they would get an additional sum assured.

Every employee was happy with this decision. My company's revenue has increased drastically to an extent which no one imagined. I have observed people's respect, satisfaction and attachment towards the company and everyone has increased their capability, skills, knowledge and experience.

Understand Life Better

During these years, I started to spend some time with myself to understand life better. Every weekend, I started visiting different places. Some of them are Hospital, Orphanage, Mental Hospital, City, Prison, Old Age Home, Museum, Library, Temples, Forests & Graveyards, etc. There are other places as well but these places gave me insights about life and made me silent from within, in those places. In silence, I was able to understand and delve deep into life. I have gone through scriptures, books, videos, movies, documentaries, research papers, psychology related references to know more about life and there are many things I have gone through to know more about life. This way, I have learned many things about life.

One day, I received a call from the CEO of an MNC. His name was Ganesh.
Ganesh: Hello Dinesh, how are you?
Dinesh: Hello Ganesh, I am good. What about you?
Ganesh: I am good. Can we meet tomorrow? I want to ask you something regarding insurance.
Dinesh: Tomorrow, I have something already scheduled but I am free from 10:00 AM to 3:00 PM. You can come anytime in between, at the place where we always meet i.e., the library.
Ganesh: I will come by 10:00 AM. Let's meet tomorrow at the library.
Dinesh: Yes, sure.
The next day, we met at the library.
Dinesh: Yes, tell me, you have some questions regarding Insurance, right?
Ganesh: Yes, I saw your policies regarding both Health Insurance and Term Insurance. I felt like you are investing a huge amount in

this without any returns as all the employees will join for one year and later they will change to another company once they get all the insurance benefits. In case their package is low, then you should decrease the sum assured so that you can save some money.

Dinesh: After listening to all this, first I laughed and said, "You will not understand why I am doing all these things."

Ganesh: Tell me, why did you do this and what is your motto behind this?

Dinesh: Instead of telling you, let me show you but I need 15 days of your time. I know how busy you are, so let me know when you have 15 days of time for me to make you understand these things.

Ganesh: 15 days, I am fully occupied for the next 1 month. Every day, I have some meetings. I cannot set aside those many days. Can you please explain to me here and now? By the way, don't you have any meetings? And if you take leave for 15 days, what about your business? Who will manage it?

Dinesh: No, it's not possible for me to explain to you here and now. In life there are some things which can be learned only by experiencing them. Regarding my free time, I have automated many things of my work and all the important decisions are taken by the respective Department heads and individual project managers. In short, **I have delegated my work**. They don't come to me until and unless it is very important and my opinion and suggestions are required. Otherwise, they do their work very well. I have full confidence and trust in them. That's why I have free time.

Ganesh: Seriously, every time I meet you; I listen and learn many new things from you. Do they have that much experience? What happens if they make wrong decisions?

Dinesh: They have more experience than me in their individual domain. Sometimes they make wrong decisions but I always say one thing to them: Learn from failures; Enhance, Upgrade and

Grow your skills and capability by thinking of multiple solutions and looking 10 steps ahead in advance. Choose the one which fits appropriately. My employees are true to themselves and others. This way, they enjoy what they are doing and even if I give them new work or alternate domains then they make it interesting and challenging because they learned that skill by understanding, observing and analyzing it.

Ganesh: I got it. I will apply some of your things and meet you when I am ready with 15 days of free time.

I received a call from Ganesh after 6 months.

Ganesh: I have free time for the next 15 days. Now at least can you show me?

Dinesh: Yes sure. Meet me tomorrow outside the library.

Ganesh: Yes sure.

We met outside the library.

Dinesh: Listen carefully, these are my instructions for our journey for the next **11 days**.

We completed that journey. In the remaining 4 days, we visited my employees' homes for 2 days. Of those 2 days, we allotted 1 day to those homes who took the benefit of health insurance, and another 1 day to those who died and took Term Insurance benefits. In the remaining 2 days, we visited Ganesh's employees' homes in the same pattern. We completed those 4 days. I said, "I hope you understand what you saw. Let's meet at the garden tomorrow, and talk about it."

Next day, we both met at the garden.

Dinesh: Now tell me, what you learned during our 11 days of journey, and what difference you have observed between your employees and my employees.

Ganesh: From those 11 days of Journey, I have learned many things about life. In simple words, "I understood life better." Now I understand about what you said during our initial conversation,

"In life there are some things which can be learned only by experiencing them".

I observed your health insurance employees are very confident without fear of any disease and they are also taking care of their health because you said to them, "**Health is the priority then work for your family and yourself. So take good care of your health. Still if you contract any illness, then I am there for you and your family to support you financially through health insurances.**" I saw love and affection shown in their actions towards you when we met the families of those employees who had availed the benefit of health insurance.

As for the employees who got Term insurance benefits, when I met their families, I saw love and affection shown in their actions towards you. It was really amazing. It was as if your employee was still alive and fulfilling his financial responsibility. I was amazed by your statement. You said to them, "**In case any incident happens and you die, at the last golden moment of life, leave your body happily and peacefully; don't worry about your family. I am there to support your family financially through term insurances**". I saw how these employees and their families are connected so deeply to you and your organization. I have never had such an experience before. The employees' children are able to complete their education without any problem and they receive a job as per their wish either in your company or in some other company, and your Training team prepares them for interviews with real-time exposure.

When I visited the homes of my employees who had taken health insurance, they were in debt after completing the treatment because the sum assured was so less as compared to hospital charges. They also have to do multiple follow ups with insurance companies and hospitals for claim settlements. Once the claim amount is over, then for that particular year the employees have to bear the hospital charges. When I visited the families of my deceased employees, I saw that they lost that person and they didn't get any benefit because I haven't opted for Term insurance and have provided only a minimum amount which is not sufficient for their family. Their children have not completed their education. Even if some completed their education, they still did not get a job, and even if they got a job, the salary is too less for them to survive. Their entire family has to start from scratch to be independent financially. If any of the family members has health issues then they cannot afford it because the employee is not working with us so they are not eligible for any of the health insurances. All their savings will go into hospital charges and in some cases, they lose that person due to their inability to afford hospital charges, and the lack of treatment will also cause some health issues in future. When I met those families, they all did not respect me and my organization. It was as if they don't respect or value me.

Thank you so much Dinesh, for showing things to me instead of telling. This way, I understand what my employee families are going through. I will definitely update my company's health insurance policy and introduce term insurances as well. This way, at least I can do something for my employees who are working for me and my organization.

Dinesh: We all are here, enjoying all these facilities because of their hard work, trust, loyalty, knowledge and experiences. It is our responsibility to pay our debt towards their loyalty, trust and hardwork. I hope you understand it now.

Ganesh: Yes, I understand very well. I am investing this huge amount with higher returns which money can't buy and understand it. Every employee is equal and important. There is no low package and high package. Every employee has a family which is dependent on them.

Dinesh: I am really very happy that you understand well what I expect.

We both hugged each other and left for the day.

Addictions

While I was researching and going through the psychology of human beings, I learned addictions also play a vital role in every human being. These are some common addictions: smartphones or laptops, internet and modern technologies, social media, alcohol, tobacco and nicotine (smoking, pan, gutka, etc), drugs (marijuana, cocaine, etc), video games on PC or mobile, gambling, sex, sleep, food (Eating), coffee or tea, exercise, shopping.

Addiction holds people's lives and they are stuck with it. There are many people who want to leave these addictions and change their life. But in most of the cases, humans want to leave these addictions but their brain is tied with it in such a way they feel like their day is incomplete without doing it because of **'Short term gratification experiences from those addictions'**. For some people it is just normal as they know their limit and for others it is an addiction because they do it excessively, which is harmful for them and their body. It totally depends on the way they balance it by thinking of it as a part of life, not as the entirety of their life. This is where addicted people need support and help from their dear ones, family and friends to overcome this addiction by concentrating and taking actions on their dreams, ambitions and goals. As per research in many cases, **"People realize the value of life after the addiction affects them and their body completely and irreversibly, and it also affects their family and friends for the rest of their life"**.

This all that I learned when I visited multiple **Rehabilitation Centres** and saw how their family is suffering without them and how they also suffer and wonder why they crossed the limit of this addiction even though their body gave them hints to realize it is still not late to work on it, to work on their addiction to change their life.

It's every individual responsibility to spend some time with themselves to be aware of addictions they have which are taking their health, time and money before it's too late.

The Incident Which Changed My Life Completely

One day, I had to attend an important meeting at a client's location which was near a hill, mountain & forest. My driver and I went there by car from Ghat roads and the scenery was very beautiful. The meeting was successful. I was on my way back home after the meeting. While my driver was driving on a Ghat road, suddenly a tree and some stones fell from the adjacent hill. It hit the car and the car fell into the deep forest valley along with my driver, Ramu. Somehow, I managed to hold on to a tree branch which saved my life for the time being. There was a forest around me. The tree branch was located 7 feet below the road and down, there was a deep forest around 500 feet further. I had held that tree branch with both hands. I could not get up and jump onto the road. The road was 7 feet up from there. I started shouting but it was a remote place so nobody was nearby and nobody was traveling by that road. I was not in a position to shout continuously. I was there for 2 days, holding that tree branch.

In those 2 days, I experienced & realized life more deeply because everything, right from the start when I got consciousness of life, memories, experiences & maturity, was all in front of me. I realized that I got these beautiful opportunities to live life but I saw I was also knowingly or unknowingly running behind business expansion, money and name, where I could understand life only a little. I didn't work enough on myself to understand and explore life in different ways to its fullest. For those 2 days, I saw myself in a desperate situation where I had 2 options, either to live or to die. To die, I had to let go of the tree branch but to live, I had to keep on holding the tree branch.

In those 2 days, everything that happened to me is taught me that this life I got is not a simple thing. It's nothing less than a miracle or an opportunity to experience and explore this beautiful life.

Most of the people take birth and live in different stages of life i.e., childhood, adulthood, young age and old age, and at the end they die. But **very few people experience and explore life to its fullest.** They enjoy every moment of life and die with a smile on their face, saying, "I utilized this beautiful opportunity and lived life." Others die without realizing what they have missed in life and wish for another life to get everything that they want because they think those things make others happy and successful.

But the reality is different. It is that every single person has to work on themselves to get clarity on what they want, why they want it, what they have to do to achieve it, what happens if they don't get it and what the alternative is. If they are really dedicated to what they want then they will take complete information about it from those who are already doing it or have it, put in efforts and take action little by little, to get what they want. Once they get that, very few people enjoy it for a long time otherwise most of them will run for another thing. At the end, they only gather things and leave empty handed. In case they die with that wish and they have their wish fulfilled, then also it's not certain that they will utilize it well to experience and explore life. They again die for a similar wish and they forget to live life. People can live with the necessary things that they need but all equipments make our life easier. Yet, there are many people who are happy without all that, but we run behind gathering unnecessary things and forget to give our precious time to ourselves, our beloved family, friends, colleagues and society.

I will explain everything that happened to me in those 2 days. I managed to hold the tree branch when my driver and my car fell into the deep forest from the Ghat Road. All my belongings, my wallet, laptop, mobile and everything else fell down with the car. The last time I checked the time it was 12:30 pm. I fell around 1:00 pm then I started shouting for hours but nobody was there to listen to me because of the remote location. I started to feel thirsty but couldn't get any water. Then after a couple of hours, I started feeling hungry. After a couple of hours, I felt my urine bladder was full and wanted to go to the toilet. Somehow, I managed to control these things. I noticed that the day was getting dark and the sun was about to set. Now again I was feeling thirsty, hungry and wanted to go to the toilet. But I couldn't get anything and couldn't do any of this.

After some time, I thought it's good to let go of the tree branch & die with the gratitude for this beautiful life and smile and say good bye to everything. It was the best thing to do because I wasn't able to control anything. But I realized I didn't live, experience and explore life to the fullest, with all its possibilities. I didn't know whether I will get another opportunity to take birth or not, after I die. I was not sure at that time then I decided to not miss out on this life at any cost till my last breath. I would hold this tree branch, whatever be the circumstances that I need to face. I saw that all the sunlight was slowly vanishing and it was slowly getting dark like evening. I was thirsty and hungry & wanted to go to the toilet. Right now the one thing that was possible to do was to urinate in my pants because my bladder was full. I thought of holding the tree branch with one hand and opening my zip with the other but I had previously tried to hold it with one hand and was unable to hold the tree branch with one hand because of my body weight. The hill was soft so I couldn't use both my legs to hold my body so that I could get some pressure relief in my hands by keeping my legs on hill rocks or holes if any. I decided to urinate in my pants because out of everything happening to me, that was the only thing in my control. I did it in my pants; both my legs were wet along with my shoes. After going to the toilet, I got some relief but still I was thirsty and hungry.

I saw there were no vehicles crossing from here. It was about to be night-time. I felt and saw there was something biting me on my face and hands. Later I realized it was mosquitos. They started to bite on my body wherever it was possible, especially near my face, hands and legs. They started to bite above my clothes also. Now it was about midnight. I did whatever was possible, to stop the mosquitoes from biting continuously. I was shaking my legs, my head and my hands in the air. Still, I was feeling thirsty and hungry. Again, I urinated in my pants. I realized many times that dying is easier than this pressure & torture. But I was going to keep my word that no matter what happened to me, I would live life. Now, I was able to see light and it was about to be morning. The mosquitos started disappearing and I got some relief. Still, I didn't see any vehicles. I was almost in a very bad situation; my hands had started painting, I was thirsty and hungry, and my whole body started to be stiff. Still I held on somehow. My eyes started to shut but I managed to keep them open. **I wished, "If I get out of here alive, then I will live life, experience it, explore it & help humanity in whatever way possible"**. It was morning time, and I went to the toilet in my pants again. I was totally in a very bad condition. Soon, it was about to be afternoon time. Now I felt it was very hot. Still, I was hoping to get some help. I started shouting slowly but I didn't get any help. In the evening, I was hungry and thirsty, and again I urinated. It was going to be nighttime and now I just thought that mosquitos would start to come and bite me again. Thinking about this, I started shouting loudly for some time and stopped. My hands were in pain.

I started to cry for I had never imagined that I would end up dying like this. Looking at the sky, I wished, **"Give me another chance to live life."** and repeated it a couple of times. Then I totally calmed down as I didn't have anything to say. As it was night-time, I started shouting for help again, thinking about the mosquitoes and my situation. Now my hands were starting to shake and were paining. Then again, I calmed down completely and I felt some cool air touching me; it was pleasing. I again shouted for help a couple of times and suddenly I heard a voice saying, **"Anybody there?"** Hearing that voice, I started crying and shouted again loudly. A person came near me after hearing my voice and he spotted me. He said, "I am alone so I'm unable to help you in your condition. Wait, I will bring some people for help. Hold on for some more time." I said, "I will hold on. Please bring them fast and help me." After some time, he brought some people and they all helped me and took me to the nearby village and I informed my family, Ramu's family and the company about this incident.

Maturity Is To Understand What Is More Important In Real Time

In that village, there was only one person who knew about plants and medicines and treating humans with them. He treated me, gave me food and asked me to take rest. That day, I slept for the entire day. Then I woke up & ate and again slept for another entire day. Again, I woke up & ate and slept for one more day as my health was in a very bad condition. After these 3 days of sleep, I was feeling good. I thanked everyone for saving me and also, I looked at the sky and thanked for giving me another chance. I said to myself, "As I've got another chance to live, I will fulfill all my promises and dreams, that is, I will live, experience and explore life to the fullest and help humanity in whatever way possible."
The person who heard my voice first came to me and introduced himself as Bharat and asked about my details and how I ended up holding the tree branch. For that I said my name was Dinesh, and I informed him about everything about that incident and how I ended up there. I asked him about his details.
Bharat: I am alone and stay in this village. I treat the people of this village and the neighboring villages using medicines made up of plants and herbs for any health issues. These are my details.
Dinesh: Next day, when I woke up I was feeling good. I roamed around the village. I observed that some strangers came into the village and asked children about Bharat for some crucial herbs and medicines they required. The children told them they knew him and asked the strangers to follow them to his house. I also followed them. Once the strangers reached his place, they gave him a list of herbs and medicines that they needed. Bharat gave them all the required medicines and herbs. The strangers gave money in return. To that, Bharat said, "**It's a natural gift to us so I don't need any money. Please use this money to plant, grow and**

save trees in your village. That's my wish." The strangers agreed to that. They gave money to those children for showing them the direction to Bharat's home. For that, one boy said, **"Don't give money to anyone. Instead of that teach them a skill which they want to learn so that they can earn their own food."** The strangers were shocked first and later agreed. Once the strangers and children went, I asked Bharat, "The boy said '**Teach a skill instead of giving money.**' That boy was mature enough at this age to know what is more important to give."

Bharat: That sentence is only a combination of some words but it changed my entire life. Now my age is 55. Five years back, I had a family. In my family, I have 2 sons. My wife had health issues and she died due to lack of treatment. Both my sons are married and they have 2 grandsons and 2 granddaughters. Most of the time my sons spend their time on their work. My daughters in law are unable to treat me as their father. Because of that, my sons always get into trouble and they had issues between them whenever I used to stay with them. I also understood they have family now and their responsibility on their shoulders. I didn't want to give them any trouble because of me. One day I told my sons, "Take leave tomorrow. We are going to our family temple. We will eat and spend the whole day there." My sons agreed to that. On the next day, we did pooja and I spent the rest of the time with my grandchildren. At the end of the day, I gathered all of them and said, **"I want to live the rest of my life for society."** I already divided the property among you and now nothing is there with me. I am taking only a couple of clothes, my wife's photo & one family photo, and some money that I had earned this month. I will leave home tomorrow. Please don't stop me and don't look for me. Don't worry, I know how to read and write so I will manage myself." At first, they cried and said sorry on behalf of their wives but later agreed to my condition.

Next day, I left home and started traveling. I used to eat at temples & gurudwaras, and sleep wherever I got some place. After a month, every day while I was sleeping, **I just wished, "I want to help people and don't want to live like this. Please show me the path."** After 1 week, when I was eating prasad at a temple, a person next to me was eating prasad and saying to another person, "There is a temple in the village **Rajaram**. Over their people get food only when they work and they teach that work for free." I asked them about that place and thanked them and God for showing the path.

I went to that temple and they took all my details. They asked me about my hobbies and working details & I told them. They said, "These are the works which are currently available: Farmer, Painter, Electrician, Gardener, Medical Helper, Cooking Helper, etc. Let us know which one you prefer." I said Medical Helper. When they asked why, I said, **"I don't want others to lose their family members because of lack of treatment."** They gave me an I-Card. When I visited the medical room, they saw my I-Card and told me these were the plants they use to make medicines for diseases. First, they showed me how they make medicines from plants and herbs. I liked it and I started doing it. In the afternoon, they called me for lunch and in the evening, they gave tea and snacks and at night they gave dinner. I was provided shelter to sleep and take baths. This continued for 1 week. In between, I went out for a walk after lunch. Now I observed everyone doing Namaskar to a lady. I saw her; her face was beautiful and there was a beautiful smile on her face even though she was aged. I asked my neighboring workers about her. They said, "There is a Board near the temple and she wrote one sentence which changed this village and her name is 'Aarti'. That sentence was, **"Don't give money to anyone. Instead of that teach them a skill which they want to learn so that they can earn their own food."** Because of that, we all are getting work and food. Everyone who knows her, respects her and greets her with Namaskar. I also started to greet her with Namaskar whenever I saw her. I worked for 1 year and learned about many medicines and herbs which can save people with proper treatment and they're free of charge.

One of my seniors told me about this place and said that we get more medicines and herbs from here. I came here & started staying here, making medicines for needy people and treating the village people freely. Using the same sentence here to make these people kind enough to help needy people and help each other. Changing generations of this village by helping them to understand what is more important. That's all from my side."

Dinesh: After listening to that conversation from Bharat, I thanked him and promised that I would also help needy people in whatever means I can. I wanted to visit that village. For that I asked the details of this village from Bharat and left the village after recovery. I realized while returning back to my family, that, **"To make a difference in people's life, I don't need to be rich, brilliant, beautiful or perfect. All I need to do is care for them with a kind heart when they are in need."**

Understand The Responsibility of Family

I visited my family and told them about this incident. I went to my driver Ramu's house with my HR Haritha and explained this incident. I expressed my condolences to his family. I said to them, "As per Employee Death benefits, you will receive all the benefits, i.e., family members will get half of the salary and your children's education cost will be borne by the company. They will be provided a job in the company. All other insurances will be there for you."

I asked them if they had received the Term Insurance Sum Assured amounting to Rs.2 Crores.

They said that they had received it. I was very happy with the Insurance support and help in this critical time.

Ramu's Wife: Thank you so much sir, for making my husband, a drunk addict, your driver. Our whole family will be indebted to you. Because of you, my husband lived and understood the responsibility of family and loved us after returning from the rehabilitation center. Now after he died, we feel financially secure with the health policy and term insurance claim amount. Thank you so much sir.

Dinesh: It's all because of my old student. No need to thank me. I am also in debt to your husband's loyalty and trust.

I left for home with my HR, Haritha.

Haritha: Hello sir, can I ask you something?

Dinesh: Yes, sure.

Haritha: Can you tell me about Ramu's story? I heard his wife saying he was a drunk addict.

Dinesh: Yes, Ramu was a drunk addict 10 years back. His son **Kapil** came to my NGO to learn about IT. The seniors taught him well. One day, I went to the NGO to get the updates on some activities. When I was about to return home, I heard someone crying. When I went there, it was Kapil. I asked him, "Why are you crying? What happened?"

Kapil: Today, again my father came home drunk, and beat me and my mother for money. My mom is a maid. I am in college. My father doesn't listen to me, my mother and others. He always comes drunk and beats us. That's why I am crying.

Dinesh: Oh, okay. Give me your father's details like where he gets alcohol, where he drank, when and why he started drinking, and what job he does.

I received all the information from Kapil and his mom about where he would be available and at what time. One day, I told Kapil's mom to make some special dish which her husband liked and that we would start eating once he came. She prepared the dinner. We waited for his father to come. After 1 hour, he came. Kapil introduced me to his father and said, "He is my professor and this is my dad Ramu. My professor was feeling hungry so I brought him here by saying that my dad's favorite dish cooked by my mom is super amazing."

Ramu: Yes, this is my favorite dish and my wife cooks well.

We all ate and I said bye to all. Left for home. Next day, I went to the wine shop where Kapil's father Ramu came to purchase alcohol and I reached 1 hour before him. I talked with the Wine shop owner. He agreed to what I said. In the shop, I was talking to the wine owner and Ramu came to purchase wine. I saw him and went outside the wine shop. I said, "Hi Ramu, how are you? What are you doing here?"

Ramu: Hi Professor, I am good. I came here to purchase Alcohol. What are you doing here?

Dinesh: The wine shop owner's son is my student and I came to talk to him.

Ramu: Okay.

Dinesh: While Ramu was purchasing alcohol, I asked how much it costed.

Ramu: It cost me Rs.200.

Dinesh: Did you get any discount on that?

Ramu: No, we don't get any discount.

Dinesh: Okay, let me try. I went inside and talked with the owner. The owner came outside and said to his employees, "For Ramu, give a 30% discount. He is our professor's friend." The employees said, "Okay sir."

Ramu was very happy and thanked me. I hugged Ramu and asked him to let me know if he needed any help.

Ramu: Yes sure. Can I call you by name, Dinesh?

Dinesh: Yes sure. Tomorrow do you have any work?

Ramu: No, I don't have work.

Dinesh: Can you come tomorrow? I have some work in an NGO where I need some help.

Ramu: Yes sure, I will come. Thank you, Dinesh. Now I feel good.

Dinesh: Is it possible for you to come without drinking? Because there are many people who will come.

Ramu: Yes sure, I will come without drinking.

Dinesh: Tomorrow, I will pick you up at 7:00 am here near the Wine shop.

Ramu: Sure, I will be ready.

Dinesh: By the way, do you have a new dress?

Ramu: Yes, I have some but they are old.

Dinesh: Okay, right now are you free. I want to take one dress for you tomorrow.

Ramu: I have one dress, no need. Thanks.

Dinesh: You are my friend, this is a gift from me. We both went to the showroom. Ramu selected the clothes. We took the clothes and left for the day.

Next day, Ramu was ready with these clothes. I brought my car and we both went to an NGO where I drove the car. The work was over. I dropped him to his home. After 2 days, again I went to a wine shop to meet Ramu. I saw Ramu was already there and he was watching a TV program. I asked him, "Do you like this program?"

Ramu: Yes, I like and love this program, especially this actor. I have a dream of meeting him and spending some time with him.

Dinesh: I saw Ramu's face when he said, "I have a dream of meeting him and spending some time with him". He was very happy and his face was glowing. I asked Ramu, "Tomorrow do you have any work? I have to go somewhere and want you to come with me."

Ramu: Okay, Dinesh. Tomorrow I will come without drinking.

Next day, we both met at a wine shop. I picked Ramu, and as usual I was driving the car. We both went to a garden. We both sat in the garden. I was doing something on my laptop. Suddenly Ramu stood up and called me. When I saw his face, he was completely shocked and very happy.

Actor: Hey, Hi dinesh. How are you?

Dinesh: Hey, Hi actor. I am good. What about you?

Actor: I am good. Now, tell me about that activity. What is the progress?

I told everything about that activity and I introduced Ramu to the actor.

Dinesh: This is my friend Ramu. Ramu's hand was shaking and his words came in a half and half, as though he was still in shock.

Ramu: Hi Actor, my name is Ramu and I am Dinesh's friend.

Actor: Hello Ramu, nice to meet you.

Now it's lunch time. Can we launch here as i arranged everything, Dinesh and Ramu?

Dinesh: Yes sure.

Ramu was silent but later said, "Yes, sure."

After lunch, I said to the actor, "Ramu is a very big fan of yours and he watches all your shows."

Actor: Is it, Ramu? I am very happy to meet you.

Ramu saw the happiness in the actor's face and the actor hugged him. He was very happy from within. The actor called the photographer and he took all the pictures. While leaving, the actor gave us one gift and said, "Open it in front of your family when you reach home."

We both said bye and again he hugged. I gave some documents to him. We both left for home. When I dropped him at the wine shop, he hugged me tightly and thanked me for the surprise. He was about to cry happy tears.

Dinesh: Don't cry, I know how you are feeling. Your wife and son also see you as a hero. So be a hero to them and take their responsibility, understand them and love them. All they want is your love. Regarding the actor, he was our NGO donor and he was planning some activity so I shared the idea and process, that's it.

Ramu started crying and said, "I want to change myself and want to be free from alcohol. Please help me."

Dinesh: Yes sure. I will help you. I am sending you to the Rehabilitation center for 3 months. They will give you proper treatment. We will meet after your treatment.

Ramu: Thank you so much, Dinesh. I am in debt to you for doing all these things.

Again he hugged me and we left for home.

Ramu: I went home and said everything about my dream and our journey to meet the actor. When I opened the gift, it was a photograph of me, Dinesh and the actor which was taken in the garden recently. I was really shocked and my respect towards that actor increased by watching his actions towards a common man and the respect he gave me. I told my family that I was going to the Rehabilitation center for the next 3 months. My wife and son hugged me tightly and started crying with happy tears. By seeing that I also cried happy tears and we all hugged each other. That day, I felt the love and live within myself. Next day, I went to the rehabilitation center. I returned home after my treatment was completed.

Dinesh was waiting for me at home. I was surprised to see him at home. I asked him for a job.

Dinesh: Anything for you, tell me which job you want to do.

Ramu: I know driving. Can I be your driver if you don't mind?

Dinesh: Sure, no problem, my friend.

This is the story, Haritha, I hope you liked it.

Haritha: It was a very amazing story, which was unheard of and unimaginable. It really inspires me and I understand why all our employees love you so much.

Dinesh: I dropped Haritha & went home.

Taking Permission Before Ending the Relationship

I gathered my family members and I said, "I have made the decision to spend the rest of my life and time to improve society in all possible ways. Till this time, I have spent time with you and worked for you as my responsibility to grow in this society. I have fulfilled all your wishes and requirements which are necessary as a parent and husband. **Now I want to live for myself.** I am always available to you whenever necessary. I want to explore myself and live in all the possible ways. In this 1 month, we will go for outings on weekends and I will discuss with you some important things. I have to resign as a CEO and I have to prepare to find an eligible one who will fulfill all my responsibilities, by discussing with the board of directors."

These are the things that I said to my wife, my children, the Board of Directors & my employees on time as per their availability.

We all family members went on outings and had our favorite food for dinner and lunch. We enjoyed it till evening. We started our conversion.

To my wife: My dear Lasya, it was a beautiful thing that you came into my life. You supported me in all possible ways; we both lived life as one. I know, I promised to you that I will be there for you till my last breath but I want to live that life which I dream of. Otherwise I will be alive but as good as dead from within. I will be always there for you in case you require me. Please grant me permission to do what I want to do. I hope you understand me.

She came closer to me and hugged me. She spoke.

Lasya: It was a beautiful opportunity to share my life with you. I will give you permission to do what you love as you always say things to us. I will live life to the fullest and explore it. I will always remember each of your words of wisdom that you shared over the period of time from our marriage till date. You will always be there with me as one even though we are physically separated and I will get in touch with you whenever I require your support and help.

To my daughter: My dear Amrutha. As you wished, I have taught you everything that I know about business in these 5 years. I think you will surpass me one day, looking at the way you learn. Now I am appointing you as the CEO which I already discussed with our company board of directors. We saw other people eligible to become CEO and compared all of them but you surpassed all of them. Now it's your call to accept it or reject it. In case you accept it then take good care of all our employees because they are all part of our family. We stand here because of their trust and support. Once you are mature enough then take a decision on your marriage then choose a wise partner & fulfill all your responsibilities. Please grant me permission & I will be always there for you in case you require me.

Amrutha: It was a beautiful opportunity to have you as my father & mentor. I always learned many things from you & you always treated me as a friend and supported us in whatever decisions we took in our different stages of life. You taught me how to make decisions, take responsibility, learn from failures & enjoy life. I will accept the CEO position & I will always take good care of our employees & support them. I will choose a wise partner for my marriage and fulfill all my responsibilities. I will grant you permission to fulfill your dreams, Dad & I will always miss you. I'll let you know in case I need your suggestions or help anywhere.

To my son: My dear Akash. I gave you everything that you require. Now you excel in your music domain. Once you mature enough to get married, choose a wise partner & fulfill all your responsibilities. Now you also please grant me permission & I will be always there for you if need be.

Akash: It was a beautiful opportunity to have you as my father & as a friend. I always learned many things from you. You always gave priority to us and our decisions. You taught us to be responsible for every decision we take and everything that we do, and to give respect to everyone. I will take music to a level that no one has imagined. I will choose a wise partner for my marriage and fulfill all my responsibilities. I grant you permission to fulfill your dreams, Dad & I will always miss you. I'll let you know in case I need your suggestions or help anywhere.

That night we ate all our favorite dishes. We remembered and recollected every moment and memory, and laughed at everything and didn't sleep the whole night. We all went back home.

I had a meeting scheduled with the board of directors in advance with proper intimation and agenda. On the day of the meeting, we all arrived at the meeting venue on time.

To the Board of directors: Hello everyone, I have already shared the details about the recent incident. I have decided to spend the rest of my life and time to explore and experience life the way I want. Now I am resigning as the CEO. Please accept my resignation letter. Over the last week, we already saw the eligible candidates for the CEO position and finalized a candidate based on the criteria for that post. Also, I have appointed the Senior advisor to our CEO; he was CEO in the past & has real time experience to deal with any challenges or milestones that the company may face in future. Please support our employees & take good care of all of them.

Board of Directors: We always respected your decision. We know if you've made a decision, it means you have given time to think & meditate on that decision based on all possible outcomes for present and future growth of this company. We request you to announce this & talk to our employees one last time about your decision.

Dinesh: I was about to tell you the same thing. Please inform & prepare for the meeting next week with our employees. I have other work to complete.

I completed my other work and now it was time to discuss with the employees.

To all Employees: It was a pleasure to work with all of you for all these years. I learned many things about business & life from you. All of you gave support & dedication to our company & me. I am really honored by the respect & trust you put in me. I have already emailed you about the incident that changed my life and it's the reason behind my resigning. We, the board of directors have decided the next CEO of the company along with one Senior advisor. Please give support and trust to our company.

I have also informed my family, board of directors & employees that as an employee of this company with CEO designation, I have gathered some amount which I am willing to spend on the rest of my life to experience and explore life. I will definitely reach out to you whenever I need your support and help. Thank you all once again for all your support.

Village Of Dreams: To Experience and Explore Life To The Fullest

I left all of them and then I visited this village. I wanted to live outside the village and I managed to make a house. For food, I started cooking on my own by doing work which I knew.

The reason why I came here is that I wanted to know more about life so I observed myself, analyzed my surroundings, started accepting things which I didn't know, questioned and meditated on those which I didn't understand or confused me. I started understanding life. I observed my entire life from the start till date by remembering and meditating on each and every moment that I had lived so far. I understood that every person goes through different stages & parts of life and they have different understanding based on their experience and knowledge. What are the common problems most of them faced & what was their solution? I wanted to make this village more ideal because during my working days, **I had a dream to make an 'Autonomous Village' which would fulfill the dreams of those who dream. In short this 'Autonomous Village' would be called the "Village of Dreams"**. I started working and writing about it by observing and meditating on it. As a CEO, I have travelled all over the world as much as possible to observe the differences and analyze how I can implement them here. Now that I have time, I can completely work on it by dedicating my life to this because it was my dream and I got a 2nd chance to fulfill & live my dream.

Vinod: Your story was really very great. I learned many things about life by just listening to it. Now as you said, you want to make this village an 'Autonomous Village' i.e., the "Village of Dreams". I am ready to help you in every possible way to fulfill that dream & **make this village ideal for this world for** experiencing and exploring life and all its possibilities to the fullest.

Important Things About Relationships

Vinod: There is one question, which has been bothering me for a while. Can I ask about it?

Dinesh: Yes, please.

Vinod: Why did you take permission from all your family members & Board of Directors? Instead of that you could have directly told them about your plans and left.

Dinesh: As a family head & company CEO, I have responsibilities for which I am accountable and I need to be always available to them. I informed them because one thing I learned in life is **"Any kind of relationship has to end one day with intimation or without intimation. Relationships can be between a couple or a family or families or friends or multiple people or any relationship."** We stay here as a family, not alone. Anything that happens to one single person in a family will affect the entire family and make them all suffer. They & their decisions and opinions are very important to me because I give value to them and respect their feelings and emotions. We have trust in each other which I have established over a period of time & they understand me very well. I can't leave them all of a sudden and without their permission. In case I left them without their permission then they would not give respect and value to me because I left them when they needed me. **"We all live in a society where one person can't live alone; he needs help and support to survive. We and society are interconnected because what society does has an impact on a single person and what a single person does has an effect on the entire society."** Not all situations and all life stages are the same. At some point in time, we need others' help and support. Simple example: We need doctor's help to come into this world and when we leave, we need some people's help to cremate.

If you don't want to help anyone, it's fine because that's up to every individual's decision but don't hurt others with personal motives because when it comes back, we realize what other people have gone through. Simple example: Your wife doesn't care about your parents, and right now she only thinks about you and your children but when the children become parents and they do the same thing then she realizes how your parents felt. At that time, it's too late to apologize.

Another thing about relationships, I have observed in many relationships.

"**If you end relationships with the permission of the person(s), then it will become a sweet memory to them for the rest of their life**". They enjoy every memory of it, even if it is a good or bad relationship. Most of the time, in a relationship there is a misunderstanding due to lack of communication between people & very few people understand other people's feelings and emotions. When any person makes a mistake knowingly or unknowingly and they have been intimidated by another person about it, the person needs to accept and apologize for it, and the other person has to forgive them. Most of the times, people keep it to themselves and their actions speak whereas in some cases people tell their mistakes to others instead of them. **They miss the simple logic that mistakes are corrected by mistake-makers by giving some time and discussion. Other people can't correct it for them."** Every relationship starts with good & sweet things and they expect this to happen throughout the relationship but things do not happen as they expected. Some challenges come in a relationship to test the relationship and their understanding of each other. But very few people understand and think about it before they enter any relationship. If there are any conflicts then open communication with each perspective will help each other to understand about things happening in a relationship.

Because of these things, **some people end relationships without any permission due to fear and lack of communication, and they are unable to face them again.** The memory for both of them will disturb them whenever they see similar memories around them. If they are deeply involved then it will disturb their entire life and in critical cases, they might go into depression.

"Before starting any relationship, always keep in mind that one day it will end irrespective of the reason". So, accept it and move on because a relationship is just one part of life and not the entire life. The reasons may be anything. For example, a person died, changed his mind because of something, had different plans which are being hindered by the relationship, etc. It could be any reason so understand another person's point of view and move on. Live your own life.

Apply the principle of 'Forget and Forgive'. It's not for them, it's for you to get peace within and move on. Just think, what would happen if you were in that position? Would you choose to end a relationship, with or without permission?

Has your question been answered?

Vinod: Yes, I understood very clearly with simple examples. Of course, I would prefer to end the relationship with permission if it is absolutely necessary to end it. Otherwise, I will go for open discussions about the problem or challenge I am facing in the relationship then we both will find a solution for it and accept the solution.

Give Another Chance to Live Life by Providing A Platform To All Those Who Deserve It And Want To Try

Tell me more about how you are going to work on fulfilling your dreams in this village.

Dinesh: **"Everybody wants to live happily and enjoy every moment of life"**. But very few people are able to really understand life and live happily. Rest all are living but they don't realize the presence of life within themselves. They live either in the past or future without understanding and seeing the whole of life. At the end of their last golden moment, they are unable to leave this body and mind with a smile on their face. They always have something at the back of their mind which they regret or something they wanted to do when they were alive but they were unable to get courage or support to do it. Other people have different circumstances or situations or responsibilities on their shoulders or some do not get resources & directions to do that work. Most of the time, they need a mentor who will guide them to do what they want to do but they cannot get one or are unable to find any mentor at that time. Everybody has their own reasons for it. I want to provide a **platform** to all those who want to try or deserve. Even if they fail after getting guidance or mentorship then they are satisfied because at least they tried & failed. I want to help them to understand and see the whole of life because everyone's life has similar stages of life but the path or direction to reach there is different for everyone. Once they understand and see their whole life then they can leave this body and mind happily with a smile on their face.

There are many things in this world which are important to work upon to improve oneself, humanity and society but after doing years of research, I found these 3 are most important to work on for every individual's happiness (Fulfilling Dreams by providing resources & mentorship):

1. Understanding of Life (Maturity of the mind)
2. Career Development (Learning)
3. Experience Sharing

I want to add and modify some things in this village. I have managed to draw the blueprint of this village. In this village, there is a place which is a combination of both forest and land. Before I add anything to it I need to own this land so that it cannot give any problem in future. To make things happen according to my blueprint, I have selected this place which will be convenient for me to add & modify things. I will also use this village land if required & modify wherever necessary as per the proper rules and regulations of this village and government. As you are already an official village head recognised by the government, I need your support to fulfill these dreams. There is one more question which might arise in future and that I want to clear at the beginning of this project: **"Why am I doing this?"** I want to live the rest of my life for society, to help needy people because it was my wish and dream to change things around me. I want to know the challenges that I will face during this process of changing things around me. While I was working on myself to understand life, I learned, **"Before we change society i.e. people, we have to change ourselves & then we can change others because fundamentally we all are the same."** From that day onwards, I have tried to change myself and understand life. **Every time I meet anyone, I look into his eyes while talking, to experience his life in his eyes.** At one point in time, I realized life is **'Divided in the united form'**. We all are connected with each other by five natural elements & love. **Once you feel a connection with others around**

you then only you will understand why I am doing all this. From tomorrow onwards, we will start this journey to make changes in people's lives so that they can **experience life within themselves and outside** so that they can **leave this body happily.**

We both left for the day & decided to meet in the morning.

Vinod: Hi Dinesh. What is the first step towards your dream?

Dinesh: Hi Vinod. I have decided to buy the land which I have located and it suits the project. We can plan everything in the initial level and we can utilize the rest of the village as and when it is required based on the villagers' demands and requirements.

We both went to see the land.

Vinod: I know who this place belongs to and he knows me very well. We can talk to him and request to sell his land.

We both went to the seller. I explained everything to the seller. He agreed to sell the land and said, "**I am very happy to sell this land for a good cause and be part of this dream.**"

I prepared an official registration paper for the sale of the land and it was completed.

Dinesh: I am very happy that the first step towards my dream is completed. Now the next step, I will explain to you. I have been preparing for this dream for a very long time. I have planned everything. I did surveys all over the world through survey agencies. This is the plan to build buildings for residences, coaching classes, conference rooms, gardens, swimming pools, sports grounds, kitchen, and everything that is required to fulfill this dream. Over a period of time, I have made some good friends who are willing to be part of this dream. One of the friends has agreed to make the entire infrastructure to fulfill all the different kinds of dreams of anyone. He is ready to give discounts as much as possible and there are some friends who donated for this dream project. The remaining amount I will pay. After 6 months, everything was ready as planned with proper approvals from the government & other authorities.

The important thing that we understood from this survey is **"gathering a target audience who has a dream and professors who can help to fulfill that dream"**. We have created the **Platform** through a web portal where everyone can register and reach out to us. This portal is available on the web & on an app. All they have to do is register themselves and provide necessary details. All the instructions are very clear and it will help those who are willing to change their life by taking action. We gave priority to students and professors in their respective fields. Students don't mean only those of age between 15 to 28 years. 'Students' means those who are willing to learn anything new or any existing thing irrespective of their age. The professors are experts in their own domain with real time experience and knowledge. For students it's free and for professors we will pay fees as per their requirements. The Portal is built on the basis of the survey and analysis that we did. It contains challenges that are faced by students, professors, industries, societies, governments, and all domains. It also contains surveys on life and all its problems.

The important thing about this program, these activities & exercises is to get clarity & awareness on **"Understanding of Life"**. Once you get clarity and your eyes are open to see the outside world and within yourself then you get to know where you stand and what you need to do to know how to make your life blossom.

3 important categories & 2 important processes: (How this program works)

Categories:

1. **Understanding of Life (Maturity of the mind)**

a. Be aware of the present moment.
b. See the whole life and the world with open eyes.

c. Be completely conscious and aware for 1 single day.
d. Every single person always wants to reach his fullest capability to live life joyfully & happily.
e. We will share the above stories and others' experiences to them to understand and experience life. They can reflect on their own life to understand life.
f. They have to do the exercises which are specified.

2. Career Development (Learning)

a. Age is just a number. All the people who are willing to learn from their heart are always welcome to fulfill their dreams with passion.
b. They are passionate about it. In the beginning they are not aware about the passion; this passion would be developed over a period of time by getting complete information, knowledge and experience about it. We call it passion only when they enjoy work without watching the time, i.e., they are totally in a different world when they are doing that work.

3. Experience Sharing

a. Rerun their own entire life experiences in front of their eyes to realize the meaning of life, awaken the self & help others by sharing their experience & giving advice to the younger generation.
b. We will record every session in both audio and video formats or they will send their recording. People will share their knowledge and experience at personal level or professional level or both.
c. The recording would be about any perspective of any part of life.
d. Anybody can share their knowledge and experience in the form of any art or the way they love to express their message (Arts: stories, paintings, music, dance, documentaries, movies, web

series or drama. People can choose multiple art forms and creative or unique ways to express their message.)
e. This can be done anywhere in the world by anybody and will be uploaded to our portal in art forms. (Privacy will be maintained if required).
f. **"By sharing your experience, you can live forever on this earth."**
g. This exercise will be in memory of a person and their contribution to this society in their absence.

Processes:

1. Before Joining
2. After Joining

Now we will go through the Processes:

Before Joining:

How this program works:
Prerequisites to enroll into the program: Offline & Online.

Do the 7 Exercises given below for the 1st week:

1st Exercise:
1. Find a convenient place to sit (Either on a chair or anywhere at any location; don't sit on the ground.)
2. Sit with your eyes open for 3 hours without blinking (Ideal: 3 hours, minimum 1 hour, maximum 5 hours) (In the beginning start with 1 minute, 2 minutes, 5 minutes and increase the duration such that you reach minimum time and later expand to ideal and maximum time.)
3. Do this for 1 week.

4. During this one week, if any external body part is moving on its own, try to take ownership of it by instructing the mind then the mind will instruct that body part. (Even though it seems like you are directly controlling a body part in a fraction of a second, the mind is involved there. Every body part should be instructed by you not by your mind. You instruct mind => mind instructs external body parts.)
5. If any body part is not in your control, first accept that it is not in your control then take your awareness there, stop it, and be calm during this process. It takes time to control all body parts with awareness. That's why this exercise is designed for 1 week with 3 hours ideal time but you can also do steps 4 & 5, all the time during this week while doing any activity.

Other 6 Exercises:
1. Maintain Eye contact while you are talking or looking at anyone.

2. Your feet must be touching the ground completely (either bare foot or use any slippers, sandals, shoes, etc) while walking or standing or sitting.
a. Recommended time: minimum 10 minutes, maximum 2 hours, recommended time :1 hour
b. Walk: While walking one leg step should touch the ground completely, then you go for the next step.
c. Standing or Sitting: Completely touch your feet to the ground and hold the same position for some time. (Experience the fact that the bottom is connected to the top i.e., the foot is connected to the mind)
d. Any Place.

3. Concentrate on your breathing. Take a deep breath in and out slowly. Look at the sky and observe one cloud at a time without blinking your eyes.
4. Try to listen to your heart beat by standing or sitting in one place in statue position. (It takes time. Try to listen to the heartbeat and if you are able to listen then try to do it for 30 minutes).
5. Give a 'pause' for 5 seconds in between any daily activity that you do & which can be paused, like reading, walking, talking, eating, or anything that is possible to pause for a few seconds.
6. You can create your own exercise. (The aim of this exercise is to experience the calmness of both body and mind which our default nature is.)

Do this Exercise in the 2nd week:

Reflection of Life:

1. Accept what you are doing currently & know why you are doing it. (that is, for survival, responsibilities, a dream, a goal or passion or out of love for it)
2. Analyze the past 1 month and how you used your 24 hours & know where you have spent your time and what are the returns. (Sometimes there are no returns; you only did it for enjoyment, fun, happiness, etc.) Plan the next 1 month then again analyze that 1 month. Continue this process.
3. What do you want to do in life? If it's decided then meditate on it & try to find **"why you want to do it"**. Do you have any reason to do it? Like you are passionate about it or love to do it or do it for survival, etc. If you don't know what you want in life then spend some time with yourself to understand. Once you have finalized what you want to do in life then go through the requirements to do that work or activity. Learn the basics of

it and get complete knowledge about that domain like its origin, history, criteria, requirements, levels, etc. by using the internet or books or videos or blogs or any source.
4. Look for the real time challenges, both physical and psychological, that you are currently facing and work on them. Analyze how much this problem or challenge is solved or reduced over the period of 1 month. (Also analyze what you did and what you didn't do.)
Repeat the exercises of both 1st & 2nd Week.

Once you get clarity then visit our place or the online portal to share your complete details. We will go through the profile and give you feedback for the next process for reaching the next milestone in achieving what you dreamt of.

To teach more about life for the first 3 months after the feedback, we take all your responsibility as much as possible, i.e., we provide a fixed amount of money to your family to survive and fulfill their basic needs in your absence. In case if you don't have any dependencies & you are financially free, then let us know.

We will take permission from your family, neighbors & friends to make you free from all your responsibilities & they can contact us in case of any emergency. If you are already doing work, take a break of 3 months if possible else if you are very determined about your dream then resign from your job. We will assure you of another job which you are passionate about or love based on your interest after **3 months of the complete program**. Mobile phones are not allowed here; we will give you necessary devices and equipment based on the requirements.

After Joining

We have divided the village into 2 parts. one part is named "Village of Dreams" where our project activities will be executed and in the other part, the rest of the village people will live as per their terms.

Blow activities in the 1st part i.e. Village of Dreams: (There are certain rules which are mandatory for everyone for **1 month**. After that, it's their choice.)

There is no alarm in this village. In the center of the village there is one long bell. Whoever wakes up before 06:00 am is are allowed to ring the bell, one ring per person from 05:45 to 06:00 am. Everyone will wake up and freshen up by 07:00 am. Once they get up then they can pray for themselves at any point in time at any place but it is recommended that they do so in their own room or if they don't wanna pray then it's their wish. They get breakfast from 07:10 am to 07:30 am. In case any one doesn't wake up then don't wake them up. Let them wake up and request to wake up by the sound of the bell ringing.

once they are free. Take a walk around the village where there are certain places which are specifically for people to walk and sit there. The places are River (R) - Water Flows continuously; Fire (F) -Fire burns continuously; Gardens (G) -They are made in such a way that people can walk, sit and spend time with trees and plants around it full of flowers & greenery. There is pure air & open sky all over the village. In the sky there are uniquely shaped clouds which are always moving very slowly. The people have to spend an hour at each location, i.e., River, Fire & Garden on all days except Sunday. On Sunday it's their choice. At 11:00 am they all have to assemble in the auditorium which is an open place. In the remaining time of the day, the Basic Fundamentals training given below is mandatory. It is already prepared & scheduled as per participants, mentors, resources & time.

Basic Fundamentals

1. **Learning English:** Grammar, Vocabulary, Reading, Writing, Listening, & Fluent Speaking. It is mandatory because to express ideas and share thoughts globally the communication should be very clear & precise. It gives clarity. (The course is already available with real time learning).
2. **Doing Farming:** To make their own food by farming on the given land so that they can understand the value of it. We will teach everything. Plant one tree and take care of it.
3. **Working in Hospitals:** Working in the nearby all village hospitals based on the criteria & available positions.
4. **Going through Knowledge Hub Information Center:** We have collected all the information from all over the world through internet, surveys and domain experts. The information is in the form of images, books, blogs, videos, etc. Everyone has to go through basic & general knowledge which is available on our platform for free. (Rules, regulations, ideas, thoughts, problems & solutions, etc.)
5. **Understand the value of Money:** It is mandatory to understand the value of money. Also, one must understand the transactions that happen all over the world and how money flows from one person to another, one state to another state, one country to another country, one business to another business, etc. Understand how different countries manage their wealth and money to survive, manage resources, for rules and regulations, etc.
6. **Cremation:** Spend some time daily at the cremation place.
7. **Cook Food:** Cook food for others so that they can learn to cook food for themselves and others.
8. **Learning Arts & Sports:** Learn any Arts & Sports that they like. It can be anything like Painting, Drawing, Music & its

instruments, Dance, Singing, Script Writing, Games, Sports, etc. (Learn a single activity or multiple one by one).
9. **Take Decisions:** Why & When to start. Once it is started then Why and How to stop.

Once the above **"Basic fundamentals"** are learned, people can choose what they want to do in the **2nd month**. We will provide study material for it in the form of theory, criteria, requirements, skills, knowledge, explanation from experts in respective domains, implementation guidance, hands-on experience & reviews.

Once that person is eligible for the job in that respective domain by learning skills, they will do an internship of 1 month in the **3rd month** otherwise they go through the learning process again until they are eligible. That person can create their own style or methodology of teaching if required. Once all the Basic Fundamentals Training and the Internship are completed then they get a certificate and later it's that person's decision to stay there and continue the job or go home and do the job. That person can educate, train and teach others the skills and knowledge that they acquired over a period of time at that time or in future so that they can be independent and learn to take their family responsibility. Give reference to others who are willing to undergo the same process because everything for the 'Before Joining' process & Knowledge Hub Information Center is available digitally with free of cost. People are requested to understand themselves to live life in a new way.

Vinod, these are the 3 important categories & 2 important processes which I am going to implement in this village to fulfill my dream.

One more important thing is that over the period of time as per requirements and needs we or the next generation will change, modify or adapt new things into the above categories and processes so that we can make this village alive i.e., make it a

"**Village of Dreams**" forever as per every generation's requirement. Even if we are not alive, our dream will live forever because we are creating this foundation.

That's all from my side, Vinod.

Vinod: I never heard and never imagined that you have this much ambition about your dreams. I am really amazed by your dedication towards this dream and the way you work on it for its implementation.

I am very happy that I am part of this dream. It was an amazing journey with you. I also learned many things about life by seeing the reality of life in every aspect and part of life. In short **"Physically we can't take anything from here but mentally we can be at peace while leaving this place, due to the way we understand and live life."**

Dinesh: You got the essence of what I meant to say.

Another Part of Naveen's Stories

Do you remember **Naveen's Stories and paintings**, Vinod?
Vinod: Yes, I do remember his amazing stories.
Dinesh: I am not sure how you will take this but there is another part of his stories which I kept intentionally out of my dream. I am currently working on it. That's why I didn't disclose it to you so far.
Vinod: You can share those stories with me, we will decide whether we need to involve those stories or not. If required, we can share the message of those stories in another way.
Dinesh: You are right. Even I am not feeling good about keeping those stories with me and letting them die with me. Let me share with you those stories and his perspective. How you respond to this is up to you.

Naveen's Stories:

Decide Life based on 2 examples

Naveen: One day I visited my friend Gyanraj's place. He was my college friend and he was from Nepal. Whenever I visited his home for any work or casually, I observed there was peace in his home. Everyone in his home was calm and silent; they treated me very gently and kindly and they respected me. They all were very happy with themselves and shared their happiness with me as well.
I went to Gyanraj's room and met him. We worked on our final year project and completed it. I went home. When I reached home, my mother was crying. I asked her, "What happened?"
Mother: Your father came home drunk and beat me for money. When I refused to give money, he beat me and took all the money.

I also told him that we are already in debt, struggling for daily earnings and our food but he didn't listen to me. Before my marriage, I used to live happily with my parents. They had very good understanding and resource management. When I got married to him, your father was a good person. For 3 years, he was a gentleman. Then he started to drink occasionally but now he is addicted. What we both expected from our marriage has totally changed. Now see what our life is like. Sometimes, I feel like going somewhere alone without telling anyone but I am unable to go because of you and your sister. I don't know when this will change and we live happily. Thinking of all this is making me cry.

Naveen: Don't worry, Mother, everything will be alright. It seems like you didn't eat so let's eat together.

I went to my room and thought about all these things. I saw how lucky Gyanraj was that his family was very unique and there was peace in their home. I was curious to know about the peace in his home. I went to his house and knocked on the door. Gyanraj opened the door and welcomed me. I went to his room and started walking to and fro. He observed me and asked, "What happened? Is everything alright?"

I said everything about the incident. I also said, "There are many families living near my house. I observed that they all fight or argue one day or the other. This is common to every family. There are some kinds of issues or misunderstandings or disagreements between them, and in case of poor and middle-class people, the major reason for this is money. Rich people also have issues or misunderstandings or disagreements but the reason may be the same or different.

Gyanraj: What exactly are you trying to say?

Naveen: I want to say, in every family the fighting or arguments happen but, in your family, I didn't observe any of these things even though we have been friends for the past 5 years. How is this possible?I want to know this.

Gyanraj laughed and said to me, "Okay I got your point. You sit first and let me bring some water for you." He brought 1 glass of water and 2 empty glasses. He gave one glass of water to me, and kept the other empty glasses as it is.

Naveen: Why did you bring 2 empty glasses?

Gyanraj: I brought them to show you something. Look at these empty glasses. In the meanwhile, I need to bring some other things.

Naveen: Okay.

I saw that Gyanraj brought some colors, a jar with water and a spoon . I said, "What are you doing?"

Gyanraj: Please look at me very carefully and listen to what I am saying then you will understand what I am trying to do.

Exercise with Glasses:

Right now, I have 2 empty glasses, a jar of water, a spoon, a Stainless Steel Pot and Special colors. All these things are made up of natural elements which are man made and come from nature.

I am doing 2 exercises in both glasses.

1st Exercise:

The 1st glass is filled with water. The water is transparent and clean. When we mix colors into water, it changes its color to the color we are mixing. When we rotate a spoon to mix colors, the form of the colours changes based on the quantity and quality of colors. We stir continuously to mix colors. When we add more water and colors into glass, at a certain point in time, the colored water comes out of glass and flows outside. When water is boiled continuously in the Stainless-Steel Pot, at a certain point in time it will evaporate. The pot will be empty and the water goes back to nature.

2nd Exercise:

Now the 2nd glass is filled with water. The water is transparent and clean. When we mix colors into water, it changes its color to the colors we are mixing. When we rotate a spoon to mix colors, at the beginning the form of the colors changes based on the quantity and quality of colors. We keep the spoon aside in a glass of water. The colors start to go down to the bottom of the glass. The water above is transparent and clean. When we add more water and colors into glass, at a certain point in time the color accumulates down and water comes out of the glass and flows outside. When water is boiled continuously in the stainless-steel pot, at a certain point in time it will evaporate. The pot will be empty and water goes back to nature.

Here are some clarifications:

Water is transparent and clean. The same way, when we are born, we are in the same condition.

Colors are thoughts, emotions, feelings, information, knowledge, experiences, memories, pain, pleasure and happiness, etc. These colors are coming from outside i.e., society (the world). (These colors are specially made in our village for this example.)

Spoon is our mind.

In the 1st example, our mind is continuously processing all thoughts, emotions, feelings, information, knowledge, experience, memories, pain, pleasure and happiness, etc. everything that comes from society through different mediums. We are not using information, knowledge, experience to understand life and analyze things around us. Our mind is not calm and stable, and because of this whatever is inside us will come outside through our actions. We have to face the reactions based on our actions. At a certain point in time, we have to die and leave this body. The body will be back to nature.

In the 2nd example, our mind is observing and questioning all thoughts, emotions, feelings, information, knowledge, experience, memories, pain, pleasure and happiness, etc. everything that comes from society through different mediums. We are using information, knowledge and experience to understand life and analyze things around us. Our mind is calm and stable, and because of this we are observing and thinking whatever is inside us, before it goes outside through our actions. We have already anticipated the reactions based on our actions because we already observe other people when they die and we are already aware that one day we die and leave this body here and our actions are based on that only. At a certain point in time, we have to die and leave this body. The body will be back to nature.

Here the 1st example is of all the people who are not aware and not understanding their life because they are running in life without thinking about what they are doing and where they are going. Their actions are happening without their involvement and they have to face the reactions based on their actions. The people around them are controlling them with their actions. If they come across any wise person who is aware of life then they feel happy with them because of their actions and they respect other people without hurting them. If they get any person who doesn't know about life then their actions are not in their control and because of this the people around them are in pain.

Here the 2nd example is of our family members.

It's up to you to decide which life you want, based on your understanding of both examples.

Naveen: I understand what you are saying but I have one question.

Gyanraj: Yes, please ask it. In the meanwhile, I'll fill the water in the glass with the jar.

Naveen: I can understand that one person is wise but how is the entire family wise? There is a huge age difference between all of them, right? Then how is it possible? And why did you fill the glass with water again?

Gyanraj laughed and said, "If there is an entire village like this, what will your reaction be then?"

I was shocked and drank that water.

Gyanraj: That water was for you. Anyway, what I said is true and it's my village in Nepal.

Naveen: Can you take me there? I want to visit your village to know more about these things.

Gyanraj: After our final exams, we have a vacation of 2 months so we will go there. Please ask permission from your father and mother so that they are aware of where you are going.

Naveen: Sure, I will take permission and we will go to your village.

We both left for the day.

I went home and told my father and my mother that I was going to Gyanraj village for this upcoming 2-month vacation after our final year exams. They didn't reply for some time. I requested them for a week and they both agreed when they both discussed with Gyanraj's parents.

Journey to Gyanraj's Village

Our final year exams ended and we both left for Gyanraj's village. I asked Gyanraj to tell me something about this village.

Gyanraj: My village is in the district of Jumla (Karnali, Nepal). Near our village there are mountains and Karnali River. There are many things which you will know after visiting our village.

Naveen: Sounds like it's a very beautiful location. Sure, I will wait and see.

We both visited his village. We both went to his uncle's home and took a rest. The next day, we both went to see the river and it was very beautiful. We visited some famous locations of his village and city. We ate all different types of food. For 1 week, we enjoyed a lot.

One day, in the morning, we both freshened up and ate food. Later I asked Gyanraj, "Can you just tell me about the fact that the entire village has wise people, which we discussed during our last discussion?"

Gyanraj: Yes, sure, but before that can you tell me, what you have observed in this 1 week?

Naveen: I observed that everybody in this village is happy and smiles when they interact with anyone. Most importantly they respect everyone, villagers, visitors and tourists. There is a statue at the start of the village. I didn't observe any cash flow in this village, which is very strange. Everyone in this village fulfills their own responsibility; no one tells what to do and what not to do. Here, we can eat whatever we want and it's free. We can't take home any food from those restaurants. In every corner of the village, crematorium grounds are there. On those grounds, there are very unique games that everyone comes and plays, irrespective of their age. All the natural resources available in this village are very well protected, like trees, plants, river, animals, birds, pets, soil, sand, land, stones, food materials, etc. For some people, the little finger of their left hand was burned. When I first saw a single person, I thought maybe he burned it during any incident but later when I visited this village, I observed many people's little finger is burned.

This is all I have observed so far.

Gyanraj: Good observation. Now I think you have already observed many important things and there are many things in this village you have not observed. Let me tell you those things and some old stories which happened in this village and it changed everything in this village.

About Tyagaraj

The statue that you saw while entering this village is of the person who is behind all the changes happened in this village. His name is **Tyagaraj**. His uncle was a traveler who shows Nepal to the tourists. After every tour was completed, his uncle came and told everything about tourism to all the children and he brought some unique things like chocolates, toys, balloons, drawing books and colors, picture books, jump ropes, whistles & piggy banks, etc. Every child in the village loved him and they listened to his stories.

One day, Tyagaraj said to his uncle, "Uncle, can I come with you?"

Uncle: I can take you with me but right now you should complete your studies as you are only 10 years old. You can come with me later.

Tyagaraj: But I didn't listen to my uncle. I told my mom that I wanted to go with Uncle. My mom talked with my uncle and my uncle agreed to take me on only weekend travels. I agreed to it.

One day, I walked into my uncle's house and said, "My studies are completed and now my age is 19. So please take me along with you on every tour. My uncle agreed. For 2 years, my uncle taught me everything about tourism, and different languages like English, Hindi, Arabic, Spanish, French and German. He taught me about famous tourist places in Nepal and other countries. I learned martial arts for safety. I became the Official Tourist Guide. Later my uncle said, "Now it's your journey. Be safe and take care of every tourist."

I started to explore Nepal and traveled all over the world with different tourists. Once a year, I visited my village for 1 month and enjoyed with my family, friends and all village people. I also brought many things to children just as my uncle did, and told stories about all the tours.

One day, when I went to my tourist agency, they had scheduled a trip to France for 1 Month. During the journey, I went to one of our agencies. Over there some tourists were talking to someone over the agency phone. I was sitting inside the agency and watching everything. I came out for fresh air and I observed one of our tourists was talking to someone over call saying, "Thank you. It was my dream to be a part of tourism and traveling. I have tried for the last 5 years, but now I got selected. Thank you, thank you so much." He left from there.

Survey on Happiest and Saddest Countries in the World

We both went to our tour bus and started our journey to see the remaining tourist places in France. During our journey, I was very curious to know about his dream which he had been waiting to fulfill for 5 years. I distributed food to all tourists and once they were all done, I went to him and said, "Hi, my name is Tyagaraj. How are you?" He said, "Hi, my name is **David**. I am good. What about you?"

Tyagaraj: I am good. I was listening to you while you were on a call. Now I am curious to know about your dream and why you have waited for 5 years.

David: Oh, okay. I will tell you about my dream. I am from Switzerland and my country is ranked in the top 10 in the "Happiest Countries Worldwide". There is one type of tourism named **"Survey on Happiest and Saddest Countries in the World"** which happens once in a year and it takes 10 months. For the 1st 5 months, they visit Happiest Countries & for the remaining 5 months, Saddest Countries. In this tourism, they select only limited people based on their objective to visit these countries. I have tried for the past 5 years, and now I have been selected. That's all about my dream.

Tyagaraj: Okay, got it. By the way, what was your objective to get selected this year?

David: For the past 5 years, I wanted to see those countries and enjoy traveling but this year I wanted to visit this place to observe and understand the differences between the happiest and saddest countries. This way I can make a report on how those countries can progress in what areas based on what I will observe during travel. They liked my objective and selected me.

For your information about GDP and criteria to select the happiest or saddest countries:

Gross domestic product (GDP) is the standard measure of the value added created through the production of goods and services in a country during a certain period. The four components of gross domestic product are personal consumption, business investment, government spending, and net exports.

To determine the world's happiest country, researchers analyzed comprehensive Gallup polling data from 149 countries for the past three years, specifically monitoring performance in six particular categories:

1. Gross domestic product per capita
2. Social support
3. Healthy life expectancy
4. Freedom to make your own life choices
5. Generosity of the general population
6. Perceptions of internal and external corruption levels

I hope you understood about GDP and why they selected me.

Tyagaraj: Thank you David, I understand very well. I am also curious to join this tourism journey. Do you have any idea how I can be part of this journey?

David: Let me check with my agency and let you know. Give me some time.

Tyagaraj: Okay sure. Thank you, David.

After 2 hours, David came to me.

David: I have talked with that agency and they said there is one option available to join.

Tyagaraj: Yes, please tell me about that option.

David: Right now all seats are full but my objective is different from others so they said that I can have one person with me to do this observation and analysis for the report. I can see how ambitious and eager you are to join this journey. I am ready to take you with me if it's okay with you.

Tyagaraj: I am absolutely okay with this. Once this journey is completed, then I will contact you.

David: Yes sure. We will meet after this journey completes. Take this Pamphlet which I have prepared and it contains everything that we need to do during our journey.

Tyagaraj: Thank you David, I will go through the Pamphlet.

I started going through the pamphlet. It had amazing questions and the observation, the standard answers to those question were also present.

Pamphlet Details:

Questions:
1. Did the Government fulfill their roles and responsibility towards their citizens?
2. Government changes the rules and regulations based on the requirements and benefits of citizens or does it follow old rules only?
3. Are the transactions transparent in the country? Government, Private Sectors, External Transactions & Citizens of the Country.
4. Be it government or a business, do they run only to earn profit or do they mean to solve people's real time problems?
5. How do people in this country manage these resources as per their responsibility: Financial resources, Human resources, Natural resources, Physical resources and Political resources?
6. Are people and Government in this country able to identify the root cause of the problem and solve it based on facts, reality and real time data?
7. People in this country follow and respect the rules and regulations of this country?

8. People in this country have Freedom to make their own life choices without hurting others?
9. People's consumption in terms of food, water, shelter, clothes, money, entertainment, medicines, etc? (Is it based on need or greed?)
10. Are people in the country healthy both physically and psychologically?
11. Do people in this country have security and respect irrespective of their occupation, designation, religion, caste, age and gender?
12. Are people in this country selfish or do they support and help each other all the time irrespective of their occupation, designation, religion, caste, age and gender?
13. People in this country are aware and understand the reality of life i.e., they live and enjoy every aspect of Life and Death. Do they welcome and celebrate Death or do they fear Death? (They live life according to the way they see death. For example, if they think they live here forever then they live one way and if they think they are guests here then they live in a different way).
14. Are people in this country aware and do they understand and experience that they are not this body and mind? Are they able to detach from body and mind? Or do they think they are this body and mind?
15. People in this country sacrifice their life and family for the welfare of society or the country or the world?
16. Are people in this country stable, calm and happy with themselves or are they searching for happiness and enjoyment outside in things and people?

Observation:

1. We will get every country's reports based on their GDP Report. We will go through it thoroughly and prepare any additional questions for respective representatives.
2. While asking these questions, make eye contact with the respective person. Observe them and their body language. It will give you clarity about their stability, confidence and truth.
3. Observe people, homes, societies, parks, roads, cities, surroundings, places and nature, etc.
4. We will go through official discussions and questions as well as unofficial ones so that we get clarity of which official is telling the truth as per unofficial discussions and their answers.
5. We will add and update things based on our observation, requirements and need to complete our survey and submit a report.
6. We will give our 100% because this will help the countries to grow for their country. If they grow, the GDP will automatically increase.

I have prepared some additional things as well for asking representatives and understand the real growth of the country.

Our France journey ended and we both decided to stay at one place till the next tour began so that we could decide and analyze more things. We took the contact details of each other and left for the day.

Next, I went to David's home and started working on the survey requirements and we brainstormed on certain topics and additional questions.

During our brainstorming and discussion, I asked David to explain this question to me. "Are people in this country aware and do they understand and experience that they are not this body and mind? Are they able to detach from body and mind? Or do they think they are this body and mind?"

David: Have you ever watched someone who died in front of you or the burning or burial of a body during cremation?

Tyagaraj: Yes, I watched someone die in front of me and others in the crematorium.

A few years back, while I was touring some place, suddenly our travel bus collided with a truck. It was the truck driver's mistake. He crossed the speed limit in the accident prone zone at the corner. His truck collided with our bus. He fell into our bus and both front glasses smashed. Some pieces of glass went inside his body and caused huge bleeding. I tried to keep him conscious but he died.

I also watched my relatives' bodies being burned and some of my friends were buried.

David: When someone dies, can you explain what exactly happens?

Tyagaraj: Let me tell you what I have heard. If anybody dies, then their body stops functioning. Their heartbeat, blood circulation, breath and all other functions slow down and stop functioning. Their bodies start to decompose. This all happens because in every body there is energy or life or a soul that is present and which people refer to by different names in different places based on their understanding. That life is us. While alive, they all have it but when they die, that life gets out of body then they die. The reason may be anything.

This is all I know, heard and observed about when somebody dies.

David: Your explanation is good. We will discuss this after our journey if you still have any questions left.

Tyagaraj: Yes sure, David.

The day had come and we started our tourism journey of **"Survey on Happiest and Saddest Countries in the World"**.

We completed our journey and we submitted our report to the respective agencies.

We both decided to stay with each other for 1 month to understand things and prepare our own satisfactory report so that in case any country wanted to change something, they could use these things to make changes.

After Discussion over 1 month, we prepared our satisfactory report.

We discussed what we observed, and this can be applicable to any place, right from a place as small as a village to one as big as a country.

Satisfactory Report for Becoming The Happiest Village Or City Or Country In The World

1. Money is a major factor which plays an important role in development. The transactions should be transparent and available to the public in all sectors, whether it be transactions from homes, government, private sectors, imports, exports, etc.
2. Money should not be yours or mine, it should be ours. This way everybody is responsible and accountable. Every village or city has a bank where all transactions happen. Nobody keeps money with them; they can withdraw or deposit money from a bank which is trackable or they should have a proper reason for having money with them ,i.e, either they paid or earned by doing any work.
3. Power should be divided equally among all representatives instead of giving to a single person. A Report Team, which contains a single representative and his team should be there to monitor everything. They don't have power and they submit reports from starting to ending on every decision and its actions. Every decision that is taken should be finalized based on facts, reality, all representatives' approval and Report Team.
4. Able to identify the root cause of the problem and solve it based on facts, reality and real time data.
5. Every single person must respect, help, support, protect and follow all rules and regulations irrespective of their age, religion, gender, occupation, designation, etc.
6. Food, hospitals, education, entertainment, homes, clothes are free of cost for everyone and all maintenance will be done by a Bank which maintains money.

7. Everyone is responsible and accountable for every resource they are using: Financial resources, human resources, natural resources, physical resources and political resources, etc.
8. Every single person should be aware, understand the reality of life and death, and be able to detach from both body and mind, then only they are eligible for any responsibility of the village or city or country.
9. They should sacrifice their life and family in extreme situations for the welfare of a village or city or country to solve real time problems by spending resources and putting in time and effort.
10. Freedom to make their own life choices for themselves or others without hurting others.
11. They should detach from body and mind and be able to prove that their actions and reactions are totally in their control as they can detach from their body by following any tried-and-tested activity or they can find any new way to detach from body and mind, which will be tested by multiple people.

This way we submitted another report again. We both left for the day and the trip ended.

When I thought about our journey, I decided to go to my village and stay there to see what was currently happening in my village and what real time challenges they were facing. I thought of solving those, telling everyone about our journey and making changes in the village so that our village would become the happiest village in the country.

I visited our village. I observed the entire village for 1 month and discussed with village people what problems they were currently facing, when the problem started, how many were impacted and since how long. I listened to every problem and went to the village head for discussion. His name was **Tribikram**. He wanted to be called by his name. So all village people called him by his name only.

Tribikram: There's a lack of resources and money in the village and from the government we are receiving only limited things. We already informed higher authorities but it's of no use. We got this reply from them: **"The king, president, prime minister and government already have other important and urgent issues in other cities and villages."**

Tyagaraj: Did you discuss with the villagers about the challenges and resources they required in Panchayat? ('Panchayat' is a council where we discuss village issues and conduct meetings.)

Tribikram: We take Panchayats on Sundays. There are very few people who come and attend Panchayats for meetings and discussion as all the people either do any other work or take rest as they work on weekdays. There is no penalty if anyone is missing. Only ward members attend the meeting and they tell about it in their wards.

Tyagaraj: Thank you Tribikram for telling all these things. I want to tell you something about my journey.

Tribikram: Yes, tell me.

I said everything about the journey, the survey that we did about the Happiest and Saddest Countries in the World, the Observations and Questions about the Pamphlet, and the Satisfactory Report to become happiest village or city or country in the world. Also I talked about my dream to make this village the happiest village in this country and the world.

Tribikram: It was a very exciting journey and all the information that you both gathered is very helpful to this world. Regarding your dream about this village, that is not so easy but all the best to you and I will give my support.

Tyagaraj: I know it is not easy but let me try. I want to know from your point of view what obstacles you think will come while implementing these things.

Tribikram: You can't change the entire village on your own. You need support and help from village people. In case you were to implement small things and it worked, let us say that by seeing your dedication, they at last agreed on helping your dream to become reality but the king, president, prime minister and government would create obstacles because if every village started wanting to change this way then nobody will listen to the king, president, prime minister and government.

One more thing is how you will manage the resources and money that are required to fulfill the needs and requirements of all the village people. How will you conduct transactions with other villages, cities and countries in the world? If you do it on your own, nobody will support you. You need to make a path where everyone is happy with your decision i.e., village people, king, president, prime minister, government, other cities and countries, etc.

The most important point among all points you specified is **"Detach from body and mind"**. If you could explain and let people experience this then everything will be on your side. It is the most difficult thing because everyone thinks they are this body and mind. One more thing which we have heard, observed and experienced in many ways is, **"Life is full of sufferings".** If you could make both things clear to people and if they could experience it then, **they can detach from body and mind. Life is all about everyone's decision about what they want from life.** If they understand and support you then things will work out your way and I hope you fulfill your dream.

Tyagaraj: Thank you Tribikram, for your point of view.

We both left for the day.

As per Tribikram, there were 2 problems in front of me. One was to detach from body and mind and the other, to understand about sufferings in life. I started to observe, understand and explore the root cause of both of these questions. Every day, I was trying to find the root cause for these problems in every situation I faced, observing others' lives to understand things, but I didn't get any insight into it. I asked some older and younger people in my village about these questions but didn't find any solution for this.

Finding Answer for One Question And Thinking About Another Question

One day, I was walking in my village. Suddenly, someone called me from behind. When I checked, it was one of my old friends, **Sanani**.

Sanani: Hello Tyagaraj, how are you? It's been a long time since we met.
Tyagaraj: Hello Sanani, I am good. What about you? Yes, it's been a long time.
Sanani: I am good. How is your tourism going on?
Tyagaraj: It is good but right now I am not going on tours anymore.
Sanani: Oh, any other plans? You love tourism, right?
Tyagaraj: Yes, I love tourism and I have different plans.
Sanani: I just wanted to know why you chose to end your work in the tourism sector which you love. What are your next plans?
I told him everything that happened during my tourism journey and about my dream to make this village the happiest village in this country and world.
Sanani: I am very happy that at least you got something in your life which is worth living for. How are you planning to implement those things in our village?
Tyagaraj: I have understood the challenges that are facing our village people and I have discussed that with our village head Tribikram. I have got 2 questions which I am currently working on, that is, "Detach from body and mind" and "Life is full of sufferings". I have already discussed those questions with the elderly and the younger people of our village but didn't find any insights about it so far.

Sanani: It's good to know that you are taking actions towards your dream. I understand that older people have already seen life so they know about it and they will share their experience and knowledge about it but I wanted to know why you are asking younger people who don't have much experience of life.

Tyagaraj: During my tourism journey, I saw many people and understood, **"Maturity has nothing to do with age. Maturity comes from hard times, mistakes, learning, understanding and experiences of life."** So I asked both older and younger people.

Sanani: I think you really changed during this tourism journey.

Tyagaraj: Yes, when I spent some time with myself and observed my actions then I found that I had changed. One more thing which I learned is **"Change is inevitable and we change continuously but people get into trouble when they stick with one thing their entire life. It may be any part of life and they do not accept the change. They have clearly seen that by changing, their life will change completely and they would be happy with the change, but still they can't let go of that one thing because the commitment to it which they developed long back, will break. Here they don't understand that life is all about living and enjoying both ups and downs in every part of life and adapting to the change."**

Sanani: Really Tyagaraj, you have completely changed. Let's come to your questions. "Detach from body and mind" and "Life is full of sufferings". These are your questions, right?

Tyagaraj: Yes.

Sanani: I think you know the answer deep down but maybe you are thinking about something else that's why you didn't find a solution for this.

Tyagaraj: Yes, you are right but how did you understand my situation?

Sanani: Your observation and understanding of life are on a different level. That's why you tell me those kinds of things about maturity and change. Now tell me about other questions which you are thinking about and afraid of.

Tyagaraj: You are right. I am finding the answer to one question and thinking about another question. The question that is bothering me is what Tribikram said, and that is "You can't change the entire village on your own, you need support and help from village people. In case you were to implement small things and they worked, let us say that by seeing your dedication, they at last agreed to help your dream to become reality, but the king, president, prime minister and government will create obstacles because if every village started wanting to change this way, then nobody will listen to the king, president, prime minister and government." In this also I am thinking about how the king, president, prime minister and government will approve my dream and allow it to become reality.

Sanani: Okay, I got your questions. Before we discuss the answers, let me tell you a story so that you can get clarity about your questions and answers.

Fundamentals of Basic Nature

There was a village in the city of Kabul, Afghanistan. There was a boy of age 15 and his name was **Abdul**. He went to the zoo everyday because his uncle worked there so he had to give him tiffin. His uncle's name was **Raashid** and he took an hour's lunch time. Abdul used to get 1 hour of free time to roam in the zoo. He was known to everyone at the zoo so nobody asked him anything.

It had been 1 year since he started giving tiffin to his uncle and watching zoo animals daily. One day he asked his uncle, "Why are these animals so lazy and inactive?"

Raashid: Instead of telling you, let me show you so that you can understand it better by observing. Next Sunday, we are going to the forest. I want you to come with me.

Abdul: Okay, Uncle. I will come.

Abdul: It was Saturday night, and I couldn't sleep because I was thinking about tomorrow. which I never saw, only saw in movies. I was really excited to see all the animals in the forest. I woke up early in the morning and got ready, then I visited my uncle's house. He took me to the Zoo and we both sat in the Zoo Vehicle. The Zoo Vehicle dropped at the forest and it took 2 hours. A forest officer came near us and my uncle talked to him. My uncle went into the forest office and brought some food and binoculars. He gave me some food to eat. I was hungry so I ate. My uncle and I walked in the forest for 10 minutes, where I saw there was a forest vehicle with the name 'Wildlife Safari' on it. I went inside and I saw it was a 15-seater vehicle and caged with iron completely so that no animals could come inside the vehicle. It was completely protected and we could see the forest clearly. The vehicle was about to start and my uncle said, "Hello Abdul, from here onwards the forest starts and it takes 3 hours to complete this journey. These are the animals which are seen by many tourists: Snow leopard, Marco Polo sheep, Siberian musk deer, Markhor, Urial, Ibex, Gray wolf, Brown bear, striped Hyenas and the Asiatic black bear. Please watch them carefully. The Wildlife safari stops for 10 minutes at every spot to see the animals in their zones. Once this is completed then we will discuss further.

Abdul: Okay Uncle. I will watch carefully.

After the journey, I and uncle went to the forest canteen for lunch. We both ate and went to a nearby tree and sat.

Raashid: Abdul, what have you observed during this journey?

Abdul: I observed these animals are happy, active and enjoying with their fellow animals. They are roaming freely wherever they want.

Raashid: Okay. Did you observe the gray wolf zone?
Abdul: Yes, I observed. I saw there was one wolf which was there in the Zoo where it was very inactive and lazy but here, I saw it was very active and enjoying itself.

Raashid: How did you identify it was the same wolf?

Abdul: Because of the yellow tag in the ear; it was still there.
Raashid: Do you know why it was brought here?

Abdul: No, I don't know. Why Uncle?

Raashid: Because it was very unhealthy and inactive. It did not eat any food for several days. At the Zoo, we decided to send it here so that it can be healthy and active.

Do you know why this wolf and other animals are so active and healthy and enjoy being here?

Abdul: No.

Raashid: Because these animals' basic nature is to roam freely with their families, be active and enjoy the forest. They are born and brought up in the forest from childhood, and they live that life only but when we bring them into the zoo, they lose their basic nature to roam freely. They are separated from their family and they are never lived in a cage because of this they are inactive, lazy and unhappy. Did you get your answer as to why these animals are so lazy and inactive?

Abdul: Yes uncle, I understand clearly. They lost their basic nature that's why they are lost to live their life in a place where they just live to survive.

Raashid: Yes, you got it. I could have told you this in the Zoo only but that would not have been effective, understandable and impactful. I thought when you observe and experience things on your own then you understand things in a better way. I hope you understand this.

Abdul: Yes uncle, I understand it very well. We both left for the Zoo, went home and left for the day.

Basic Nature of Human Beings

The next day, I woke up and told everything about yesterday's journey to my mom. She said, "Okay." I said, "Mom, last night, I was not able to sleep properly."

Mom: What happened? Is everything alright?

Abdul: Actually, I was thinking about the basic nature of human beings.

Mom: To be true, even I don't know. Let me tell you what I know about it. As a human being you get questions like, "I am a human being then why don't I know about basic nature?" You are right. We are human beings and mostly everyone here is just living to survive and provide themselves and their family with a good standard of life. Most of the people don't think about the basic nature of humans; they just live life based on their needs, desires, requirements, thoughts and emotions. In the survival process they need food, clothes, shelter and protection. We need family to survive, and family doesn't mean only mom, father, grandparents, siblings, etc. By default, most of us get a family, but there are some people, such as orphans, who, irrespective of their age, don't have this kind of family. Everyone has a choice to make their family without any limits and boundaries by helping, caring, loving, enjoying with other beings. Once they have their basic survival sorted then some people think and work on their dreams and goals that are either personal or social. Some achieve them and some don't. It's truly based on putting in their efforts, time, resources, consistency and patience. If they don't have basic survival then they work for it for their entire life. This is all I know.

Abdul: I understand a little bit but still this is not a satisfactory answer to my question.

Mom: Do one thing; go and ask this question to Raashid's wife, your Aunt **Mabella.**

Abdul: Okay, Mom. I will go and ask. Thank you, Mom, for everything.

Abdul: Hello Aunty, how are you?

Aunty: Hello Abdul, I am good. What about you?

Abdul: I am good, Aunty.

Aunty: Okay, take this snack. Uncle told me about your question and journey. By the way, your uncle already took a tiffin box today with him.

Abdul: Thank you for the snack and it was very interesting to experience those things. Aunty, I have one question. Can I ask you?

Aunty: Yes, Abdul. You can ask.

Abdul: This is my question: "What is the basic nature of human beings?" And when I asked my mom, this is what she said and she told me to ask you.

Aunty: I got it. Every human being has to go through a survival process by default. That is all your mom said, which is just the beginning. **"The basic nature of human beings is to live happily** and peacefully, doing something which is effortless and timeless and makes them happy from within."

Abdul: Could you please elaborate more because I didn't understand?

Aunty (Laughs): I knew it from your face. Okay instead of telling you let me give you a task of 6 months. Are you ready to do it?

Abdul: Yes, Aunty. I am ready and excited for this.

Aunty: Your college is in the morning from 7:00 am to 11:00 am, right?

Abdul: Yes, Aunty. You are right.

Aunty: What do you do after that?

Abdul: I give tiffin to uncle Raashid. Later I do temporary work here and there for my education and family.

Aunty: How much do you earn there in a month?
Abdul: On an average, 5000 Afghani.

Journey to Observe and Experience with Painters

Aunty: Okay. For the next 6 months you will be staying with 3 different painters; two months with each. In the morning you go to college, then after that you will help those painters till night and you can sleep there. They will give you food and clothes. Per month they will give you 3000 Afghani and remaining 2000 Afghani in the form of food and clothes. Is this okay for you?

Abdul: Yes, Aunty.

Aunty: I will talk to them and from next month you can start. Regarding giving tiffin to your uncle, I will manage that. I will talk with your parents.

Abdul: Okay Aunty. What exactly do I need to do?

Aunty: You are going there as a helper so you have to just do what they say. There are some instructions for you.

1. Observe them closely, especially their words, actions, and face. (The actions include how they are talking with their clients, family members, employees, etc. Know their employees' background and ask them questions if required, like about their paintings, their boss, etc.)

2. Understand their painting business, which means how do they work and how do they earn.
3. When they are painting, watch them very carefully, and ask them to show their personal paintings when they are free.

4. Ask them questions if you have any, but mostly observe. You will get your answers but you can ask them if you don't understand something.

5. There is one condition: you don't tell them anything about your questions and journey.

Are my instructions clear to you?

Abdul: Yes Aunty. Can I ask you something?

Aunty: Yes.

Abdul: How do you know them?

Aunty: I was doing work with them for my family to survive.

Abdul: Okay.

Aunty: We will talk after 7 months.

Abdul: After 6 months, right?

Aunty: After 6 months, your task will be complete but I want you to reanalyze those moments and memories once again for the next 1 month to find the answer to your question. During this journey, you will get more questions so try to understand those questions and find answers. Is it clear that we will discuss it after 7 months?
Abdul: Yes, Aunty. It is clear.

We both met after 7 months.

Abdul: Hello Aunty? How are you?

Aunty: I am good. What about you? Take this snack I have just made.

Abdul: I am good. Thank you, Aunty, for the snack.

Aunty: Can we start, Abdul, about your journey of Observing and your Experiences with Painters?

Abdul: Yes Aunty, Sure.

Let's begin.

Painter 1:

Abdul: His name is **Ahmad**. When I visited him, he asked about you. I told everything about you. He was very happy.

Ahmad: Why exactly did you come here?

Abdul: To learn painting and earn some money for my college and home.

Ahmad: Okay, fine. I will teach you everything I know about painting.

Abdul: I started observing him for 2 months continuously.
His words and actions were totally different. He says good things to his family members, gives commitment to clients and casually talks to employees. But when it comes to actions, he doesn't understand his family members; he only wants his family to listen to him and he doesn't give them freedom to make decisions, time to understand them and money to spend where they want. He gives money to them only when he thinks it is required.

He gives more commitment to his clients; however, he doesn't fulfil his commitment. Out of 10 times he only fulfilled his commitment twice. The remaining 8 times, he broke his commitment and delayed it or the quality of painting and equipment was not that good. When I asked his employees about him, most of them said he is a good person but the problem with him is that he doesn't think about others. He does what he thinks right. He always ends up breaking his commitments with clients and us because **his plans and ideas to run a business are always based on his imagination and he doesn't think about reality and facts**. He always takes up more work than the resources available, and because of this we always end up doing extra working hours. I asked his employees if are they satisfied with his paintings. They said, "No, we are not satisfied because we don't get quality painting products and tools, and time to complete paintings. We are always in a hurry to complete the paintings because of deadlines."

One day when I saw that Ahmad was free, I asked him about his painting business and how he earns from it.

Ahmad: I have painting shops in main cities. We take orders from people both online and offline. We go through the latest trends and paint them. We do all types of painting works.

Abdul: Do you have any personal paintings and nowadays are you painting anything?

Ahmad: Yes, I have some personal paintings which I did long back and nowadays I am busy with my business so I haven't had time to paint anything.

Abdul: Yes, I can understand. Let me see those paintings. When I saw those paintings, I asked him, "Do these paintings have any meaning?"

Ahmad: Yes, some have a meaning which is written on their back and some I paint in general.

Abdul: Ok.

I saw the paintings which had meaning, and other general paintings as well. He told me some of the painting basics.

Painter 2:

Abdul: Her name is **Zoya**. When I visited her, she also asked about you. I told everything about you. She was very happy and told me that you were her first assistant in painting.

Zoya: Why exactly did you come here?

Abdul: To learn painting and earn some money for my college and home.

Zoya: Okay, fine. I will teach you everything I know about painting.

Abdul: I started observing her for 2 months continuously.

Her words and actions were totally in sync. She takes care of her family members, gives commitment to clients and casually talks with employees. But when it comes to actions...

She understands her family members very well. She has patience and explains to her family members when they are in trouble by counter questioning them to change their perspective. She listens to her family members and gives them freedom to make their own decisions by taking complete responsibility for it. She gives them time, support and help when required. She gives them money to invest in themselves for growth. She says, **"Money can be earned again but time will not come again so use it wisely with longer vision and plans which should be based on reality and facts."**

She makes exact client commitments that she can fulfill. She goes through the requirements and discusses with the clients so that they both agree on the outcomes. She always adds 3 days in advance to every commitment. She always delivers paintings on time with good quality. Out of 10 times she fulfilled her commitment 8 times, and the 2 times she was unable to fulfill, it was because of the client's last moment change in requirement. When I asked her employees about her, most of them said that she is a very kind person and she thinks about them. She always thinks from a different perspective before concluding or taking any decision. She always completes her commitments with clients and us because **"Her plans and ideas to run business are always based on reality and facts"**. She always takes work based on the available resources because of this her employees are always able to complete their work before the deadline. I asked her employees, "Are you satisfied with her paintings?" They said, "Yes, we are very much satisfied with every painting we do because we get quality painting products and tools, and time to complete paintings. In some cases, we give our ideas and our perspectives about paintings to take the work to the next level. She and our team think about it and if it is worth adding then she compliments us and gives permission to add. We always get extra time after completing the paintings before deadlines. We use that extra time and we get extra days of no work where we upgrade our skills, knowledge about painting, and technology for the same. We have our own unique collections which we prepare for Art Galleries and Painting Competitions at National & International Level."

One day when I saw that Zoya was free, I asked her about her painting business and how she earns from it.

Zoya: I have painting shops in main cities and some villages. We take orders from companies and customers both online and offline. We go through the latest trends and create our own trends. We do only specific types of painting works because we are masters in that specific type of painting only. We earn a good amount of money from that.

Abdul: Why don't you take all types of painting works?

Zoya: Before I started my business, I did market research on all types of painting styles at both national and international level. I studied painters' autobiographies and went through all the paintings of history and till date. I went through many Art galleries, Competitions, World Records like Guinness World Records, other countries' records, etc. I found out about the top business, Galleries and Companies in Paintings and the background of their Director and CEO, i.e, why they came into this field, what achievements they did, what their yearly company income, growth and revenue were. I researched scope for the different paintings in future based on available information and knowledge. I identified genuine painting courses available offline and online by going through the teachers' achievements, skills, knowledge and experience, as well as reviews from old students and their current status after completing the course.

After doing all these things, I spent two months on different styles of paintings. I found that we can't be professional experts in all types. Later I observed, identified and decided this style suits me as per my basic nature.

Abdul: Okay got it. Can you tell me something about basic nature? How did you identify your basic nature?

Zoya: Let me tell you what I know about it and how I identified my basic nature.
Every human being wants to be happy and at peace. In this life there are many ups and downs that will come in many forms from any part of life to teach us about life. Life is a combination of all ups, downs, mysteries, thrills, suspense, tragedies, pains and pleasures, etc. Life is the art of living, learning, and growing through all these things with happiness, peace and a smile, by seeing the whole of life. The most important thing about life is to see our whole life and that of others by observing their life. Then you decide what you want from life. For convenience, I have divided life into multiple parts based on common phases so that one part of life couldn't disturb other parts of life in the worst situations.
Everyone has their own choice to decide what they want from life from every part of life or whole life.
These are the common phases of life every human goes through, i.e., childhood, teenage, adulthood and old age.
In these phases there are many parts of life which are new to everyone and will introduce life to you in that part. But the problem here is the expectations, limitations, criteria that we set. Expectations are based on our imagination of what we want and it is based on the information and knowledge that we have. The reality of that part of life is totally different from what our expectation is. That's why we suffer in pain and break in that part

of life because it shows us the reality of that part of life which is totally opposite to our expectations. The best part of living life is seeing the reality of life based on facts, past, present, and truth.

These are the different parts of life which I have researched and divided, based on human life:

"Physical health, mental health, emotional & inner well-being, family and friends, education & career, professional life, financial freedom, relationships, social life, environment & contribution, adventures, fun, passion & creative life, personal life (spend time with self), spirituality (to experience self & to understand more about life by seeing reality of life), values and truth."

Once you understand and observe these things in your life and in the lives of others who are living with you or have passed away, then you learn something from it like, "How they wanted to live and how they lived", "What are the things they did not learn and accept" and "What actions and efforts they didn't put to get what they want, as they just dreamed about it". Once they see all these realities of life then they get clarity and accept the fact that **"They don't know how much time they have to live life then they spend every moment of life, every day with a new beginning of life which is worth living."** Once you are aware and see the reality of life then you see your common basic nature from all these things, i.e., every part of life and in all phases. Then your basic nature will reveal itself to you. It changes over a period of time with maturity and understanding of life, but the basic fundamentals of basic nature will be the same, i.e., to live happily by watching all phases and parts, doing something which makes them happy from within so that they can live their life the way they want.

I hope you understand, Abdul.

Abdul: Some things I understood but some, I didn't.

Zoya: Don't worry when the right time comes, you will understand everything. The right time comes when you observe the reality of life through your life experiences and others' life experiences.

Abdul: Okay. I wanted to ask you about other things. Do you have any personal paintings and nowadays are you painting anything?

Zoya: Yes, I have some personal paintings and nowadays I am painting once in a month because it takes time to complete them.

Abdul: Yes, I can understand that. When you are in a flow then you can complete that painting but sometimes other important things come up, which make you delay in completing painting. Let me see those paintings.

When I saw those paintings, I said, "These are the most beautiful paintings I have ever seen and every painting has its own meaning. Every painting speaks something.
Where do you paint these paintings?"

Zoya: Mostly at home, and sometimes at shops & art galleries. By the way, what do you observe in those paintings?

Abdul: The phases of life and different parts of life are beautifully painted. There are some other paintings which are very beautiful and make me feel happy from within.

Zoya: Right now, what you are understanding is totally based on your knowledge and experience but there are other meanings hidden in these paintings which you can understand once you change your perspective and experience life.

For example: See a painting or a movie and then see it again after a gap of 1 year then you will be able understand what I am saying. The story behind that painting will change from person to person. In movies, you understand every cast has its own different story.

Abdul: Yes, I can relate to it.

Later she told me some of the basics of painting. Then I said goodbye to her at the end of the 2nd month and left from there to go to the next painter.

Painter 3:

Abdul: His name is **Shehzad**. When I visited him, he also asked about you. I told everything about you. He was very happy about you and he said he misses your 'Kabuli Palaw' dish.

Shehzad: Why exactly did you come here?

Abdul: To learn painting and earn some money for my college and home.

Shehzad: Okay, fine. I will teach you everything I know about painting.

Abdul: I started observing him for 2 months continuously.
His words and actions were totally in sync. Later I was shocked to see that he was similar to Zoya in every aspect. For 1 month, I was there in his office to observe his employees and business. The differences which I observed in his painting styles for the business were very unique and different. His employees take care of his entire business. They said he only participates when there are very important meetings with clients that are monthly or quarterly.

The next month he took me to his house. He has hobbies like Buzkashi, Golf and Skating.

One day when I saw that Shehzad was free, I asked him about his painting business, how he earns from it and why his employees ran his business.

Shehzad: I have painting shops in the main cities, some villages and other countries. We take orders from Art Galleries, companies, and people via both online and offline modes. We go through the reason behind the painting request, and the requirements, then we research it. We compare all old paintings of that category then we create our own style of unique painting. I gave my staff full freedom and choice to decide which painting style they want to master. I arranged every resource that is required to learn that skill from all over the world. In some cases, I send my employees to other countries to learn that painting style. Right now, I have 10 different styles of painting teams in my business. My team takes care of the earnings from the business. I trust my employees and that's why they run this business.

I take care of my employees' families, health issues, their children's education etc. That's why they trust me and I trust them. I say only one thing to them, "Take your time but give your 100% at work. Instead of doing 10 things imperfectly, do one thing perfectly." My employees don't work for a salary; they work because they love doing it and enjoy every painting they make.

Abdul: You are 40 years old, right? And you are financially free and you have free time to do other things. I have seen people work their entire life but still they are neither free financially nor personally.

Shehzad: Yes, my age is 40 and I am free. I do other things, which makes me happy from within, as I live every moment of life to its fullest possibility because I know one thing for sure: I have this life in my hands so I have decided to live it.

It is possible for everyone to get financial freedom and time freedom.

Financial Freedom

The most important thing in life is to know that we have only one life in our hands. People should spend some time with themself to identify and decide what kind of life they want to live, and what makes them happy from within and seems effortless and timeless when they are doing it. If they identify that, then they can make their career in those fields. If they are not able to identify then they have to explore every field in this country and the world by researching about it by going through the Internet or books or videos about it and learning from the experts of that domain. They should see the reality and facts about that field and research about current and future positions. Later they can decide in which field they want to pursue their career or create their own field by understanding the gap of that field. First learn the basics of it either from genuine experts, online or offline. The more the information, knowledge and experience you get, the more you will enjoy that domain. When you do that work, if you observe yourself, you can see where you enjoy from within and you give complete focus and attention to it. In short when you are completely involved in it, forgetting everything around, and you work irrespective of the time, then you are truly enjoying. This you can know within 2 months or 6 months.

Once people make this their top priority then they can achieve it by starting it by taking small actions. Now you start to prepare step by step plans and goals which are specific, quantifiable, feasible, and based on reality, facts and research about that domain or field. Here they have to put in all their efforts, time, resources, and dedication to do consistently by analyzing weekly, monthly, quarterly and yearly checklists. Modify the checklist based on the actions, progress, growth and results.

The above one is about earning by doing work. Now people should also be aware of where they have to spend and where they don't have to, and how they can make other passive incomes without doing anything. Research more about it and you will get other details.

Time Freedom

To get time freedom, all you have to do is delegate the work and automate your job or business in such a way that work should be complete without your presence. You should be present when it is absolutely necessary, like weekly or monthly.

To delegate any work to other employees you should respect, care and trust them so as to be able to see their hidden potential to do that work and teach them how it can be done in the most efficient way with limited resources. You can also appoint others who are passionate about it at that position. In short, it's their dream and they already achieve other dreams and milestones which they dream.

To automate, you have to identify the technologies and resources to delegate in such a way that your work can be complete without your presence.

This is not done in just a few months or a year; it takes time. You have to accept things and failures from others. Patiently teach and correct them. In some situations, ups and downs are bound to occur, so learn from it and grow from it. This way you can get freedom from financial stress, and you get more time to do something worth doing for society and humanity.

Most importantly everyone has 24 hours a day; all they have to do is analyze where they are using their time. Once they analyze, they can get an idea of where they are spending their time unnecessarily. From there, they can shift it in such a way they get returns or grow in their career. This way they can decide where they want to use their precious time. If they are consistent, then over the month, they can see the results that they are going toward where they want to go in life.

One more thing, if you do business then the most important thing is to decide your target audience or consumers. If you do a job then the most important thing is to decide your domain or the company where you want to work, and where your skills are acknowledged and respected. Otherwise, you end up on the wrong side of the story.

Example: "Understand life, then create your worth by spending time with yourself, then identify where you are needed and go there. Then they will understand and recognize your worth."
Is it clear, Abdul?

Abdul: Yes, it's clear. Can you tell me something about making work effortless and timeless?

Shehzad: Yes sure.

Effortless: At the initial level, you need to have the desire to identify and decide why you want to learn and what you have to learn. Once this is clear then you start to get information and knowledge about the skill or domain or field related to that work. Once you get genuine and proper information from the Internet, books, videos, research and domain experts, then you can decide to learn that skill by implementing at a small scale. At the beginning it takes time to learn and acquire that skill. The more the information and knowledge you get, the more the interest and passion you will develop towards that work by implementing practically. Once you implement it practically then only you understand where you stand and what needs to be done to become an expert. The more the experience you get, the more the expertise you develop over a period of time then you do that work effortlessly.

Example: To do work effortlessly in 10 minutes you need 10 years of working experience. (It all varies from person to person based on the skills and knowledge they acquire along with experience.)

Timeless: Once you love and enjoy what you are doing then you will be happy within. First find meaning, understand how your work is helping people to solve their problems and understand your company's mission and vision in life as well as your own. Once you love what you are doing then you put in all your efforts, attention and dedication to get completely involved in your work. Then your hours of time will pass very quickly, making your work timeless.
I hope you understood both 'Effortless' and 'Timeless'.

Abdul: Yes, I understood. I wanted to ask you about other things. Do you have any personal paintings and nowadays are you painting anything?
Shehzad: Yes, I have some personal paintings. And I have been painting once a month or sometimes once a year because I am looking for more challenges in different sectors.

Abdul: Yes, I understand that. When you have something within you, you do paintings. Let me see those paintings.

These are the most beautiful paintings I have ever seen and every painting has its own meaning. Every painting speaks something very unique.

Shehzad: What did you observe from these paintings?

Abdul: The entire book's important modules are portrayed in these paintings. History of countries is summarized in other paintings; I saw there are some famous personalities whose stories or autobiographies are portrayed. They're really very unique paintings. I used to think that people only paint certain objects, but you have portrayed so much other than the objects with your brush and various colors.

To see the whole life of a human being, you created a 100-year calendar for that person when they are born so that they see all the phases and different parts of life. A complete story.

Shehzad: You really observed well. When you love what you do from deep within, then you put everything into it and this creates masterpieces that are totally on a different level.

Abdul: Where do you paint these paintings?
Shehzad: I prefer open natural places like beaches, forests, hills, mountains, etc. I travel to different parts of the world to get my unique and different themes then I paint over there. Some I keep in the Art Galleries in that country and some I keep to myself.

Abdul: That's why these paintings are totally next-level.

I thanked him. Later he told me some of the painting basics. At the end of the second month, I bid him goodbye and left.

As you said, in the 7th month when I reanalysed those moments and memories, I found the answer to my question. I also saw that the 1st painter was not aware of life, that's why he was not stable but the remaining two painters were aware of life, that's why they both are very stable and up to the point. They both know exactly what they are doing, maintain eye contact, respect every one, are able to sit alone for hours, are extraordinary in their domain, and understand the value of life, people in their life, money and other things very well.

This is all about the journey of Observing and having Experiences with Painters.

Aunty: You really observed very well. Did you found the answer to your question, "What is the basic nature of human beings,"?

Abdul: Yes Aunty, I found the answer to my question with live examples and experiences.

Aunty: I could have told you this when you came here but that wouldn't be effective, understandable and impactful for you. I thought when you observe and experience things on your own then you understand things in a better way. I hope you understand this.

Abdul: Yes Aunty, I understand it well. Now it's clear to me that I want to do something in life which is worth living for and I will identify and decide the path to reach where I want to go.

Sanani: Now, the story about Fundamentals of Basic Nature ends. Did you get the answers to your questions, Tyagaraj?

Tyagaraj: Yes, I got the answers. I need to get Financial Freedom and Time Freedom so that I can do what I want to do. I need to focus on my target audience. Let me see if these villagers are ready to change and accept new things. If they are not, then there is no use in spending my life here to change them. Life has four phases and different parts of life.

Freedom From Suffering

When I analyzed these stories, I found that life is full of suffering because of our expectations, criteria and limits that we set based on our imagination. Most of the people don't want to see and accept the reality of life i.e., birth, life & death. They think they will live here forever. That's why they make their own imaginary world and they suffer. Once they accept life and see the life of themselves, others, and those who have passed away, then they observe they are not this body and mind. Once these things are clear and then they are aware that they are not this body and mind then they see the body and mind is suffering but they observe as an observer and this suffering will no longer disturb them.

Sanani: You got it Tyagaraj. As you have another question from Tribikram, what are your plans next?

Tyagaraj: Let me spend some time with myself to understand things at a deeper level and let me find a way to get freedom in terms of both money and time. Until and unless I am free, how I can free others? Most people say, **"First you do, then set an example for us so that we can follow you."**

We both ended our conversation and I thanked Sanani for sharing those stories which gave me more insights. We both left for the day.

For the 1st week I didn't understand what exactly I needed to do but it was clear that I needed to do this at any cost. One day I went to Karnali River for a bath. After the bath I decided to close my eyes and experience the river and its surroundings through my heart and senses. I was able to listen to the flow of water and the chirping of birds.

My body was able to feel cool air which was flowing and I was able to experience calm, peace and silence within. I did this for 2 days. On the 3rd day, when I started doing this, suddenly I started recollecting everything in front of me from my meeting with David till date, including the story of 'Fundamentals of Basic Nature'. Each and every moment and word, I observed again one by one.

After doing it 5 times, 3 things were very clear to me.

1. I Need to "Detach from body and mind" first and then I need to find ways for others to detach.
2. Get financial freedom so that I am able to reconstruct the entire village.
3. Get approval from the king, president, prime minister, government and village.

Understanding Jumping Process of Thought and Memory

During this process of recollecting everything, as soon as I became aware of my thoughts and memories, I started going from that thought to older previous connected thoughts., for example, I was thinking from A to Z in ascending order and when I became aware at point P, I started going back in descending from P to A and reflected on when the thought started and why. This way, I did 4 to 5 times. Now I was in a position to see my thoughts and memories and observe how I was going from one thought to another as one memory is connected to another. Understanding jumping process of thought and memory. During this process, I identified that there is no thought without any word. Every thought starts with words and our mind thinks it in images.

I started to work on these things. One day, one of my friend's mom died due to old age. I went there and supported my friend in all the rituals. When I went to the crematorium, all was set for the funeral. I observed from the beginning of the burning till the end. In the middle of burning, suddenly I experienced a sensation of burning in that place. There was a strange feeling that came to me and made me feel empty within. My eyes were open without blinking and were watching me burning in that place. I wanted to go outside and leave from there but my legs, even though completely touching the ground, were not moving at all. It was like my legs were attached to the ground. I thought, "Why am I getting scared? This is reality and a part of life which everyone has to go through. If I am scared now and don't face this death now, then I will never face it again. This opportunity will never come again in my life so let me face it and stand still till the end of the burning."

Once the burning was completed, there was one question which was bothering me, "Why crematoriums are always either outside of the village or at abandoned places? Why not every corner of the village" everyone has to come here irrespective of gender, age, who they are and what they do. "Why didn't everyone see themselves in that burning place and experience death".

After everything was finished, my other friend came near and shook me and asked, "What happened and what are you thinking?" Everybody started to go home, let's go home. I said, "Nothing, let's go home."

That night, I got the most peaceful sleep.

Next day, I went to Karnali River for a bath. This time, my legs were completely attached to the ground and I wanted to move but my legs were not ready to move. I stood like a statue for an hour and my eyes were open without blinking. I did this for a week. Then the duration increased to 5 hours. During this exercise, I felt like my body parts are connected i.e., "my bottom is connected to the top" because my mind started to calm down and get stable. I was able to see my internal thoughts, emotions and external things clearly.

Now I repeated those 3 questions. Slowly, I was able to see some insights into those questions. After a year, I prepared and implemented things on my own for both questions. It was working.

Detach From Body and Mind: (Let Me Tell You What I Did to Detach)

1. I understand and observe the process of birth, life & death (from myself, others and those who passed away). The difference between a live body and dead body is, both contain body and mind but in a live body it is active and controlled by you whereas in a dead body it is inactive for, the You is missing from that body and mind. Once these things are clear then we accept the truth of life that we are guests here who take birth, live and die. Once we accept life and see the life of ourselves, others and those who have passed then we observe we are not this body and mind. We are doing all these things to experience the self through this body and mind. (Understanding that I am not this body and mind is important for detachment).

2. I am able to see and observe my body whenever it hurts physically knowingly or unknowingly. At that time, I am watching my body get hurt without reacting to it because I am aware that my body and I are different. Later, I diagnose my body and get treatment for safety. This helps me to understand and experience the separation between my body and me.

3. There are two important things that help me to live the present moment in the initial level i.e., eyes & breath.

a. Eye contact is a very important thing which helps me to live in the present moment.

b. I maintain eye contact while talking to everyone. This will help me to experience myself and others' presence through my eyes.

c. See the whole of life and the world with open eyes without blinking.

d. Breathing is an important process of human life which connects both mind and body.

e. Concentrate on Breath. (Take a deep breath in and out slowly) Look at the sky and observe one cloud at a time without blinking your eyes.

4. Statue Position: My eyes were open without blinking and my legs were completely touching the ground and not moving at all in standing position. It was as though my legs were attached to the ground. During this process, I experienced that my Bottom is connected to the Top. (Tried with bare feet or with slippers, sandals, shoes, etc. while walking, standing or sitting).

a. Recommended time: Minimum:10 minutes, maximum:2 hours, recommended:1 hour

b. Walk: While walking, one leg touches the ground completely then go for the next step.

c. Standing or Sitting: Completely touch your feet to the ground and hold the same position for some time at your convenient place. (Experience that the bottom is connected to the top i.e., foot is connected to mind.)

5. Aware of mind and body: (This is helping me to understand and experience the separation between my mind and me because I am aware of my body parts working during activities).

a. For one week, during any activity if any of my body parts is moving on its own, I try to take ownership of it by instructing the mind then the mind will instruct that body part. (Even though it seems like I am directly controlling a body part in a fraction of a second, the mind is involved there. Every body part should be instructed by me not by my mind. I instruct the mind; the mind instructs body parts.)

b. If any body part is not in my control, first, I accept that it is not in my control then I take my awareness there, stop it, and I am calm during this process. It takes time to control all body parts. That's why this exercise is designed for 1 week while doing any activity.

c. Whatever is there inside of me will come outside through actions. It will flow through emotions, thoughts, feelings, love, happiness and smiles, etc. I make sure to be aware of what is inside by spending some time with myself.

6. Try to listen to the heart beat by standing or sitting in one place. i.e., in statue position. (It takes time. Try to listen to the heartbeat and if you are able to listen then try to do it for 30 minutes).

7. Give a pause for 5 seconds in between any daily activity that you do, like reading, walking, talking, eating, or anything that is possible to pause for a few seconds.

8. I started walking deep into the water, carrying weight on my hands till my breath supported it.

9. You can create your own exercise. (The aim of this exercise is to detach from both body and mind).

Get Financial Freedom To Reconstruct The Entire Village

During my tourism work, I saved some money. I analyzed what I could do to earn. One work was tourism which I could do by modifying some things in the village to attract the tourists and show them the village. While traveling, I observed different countries and what they were doing to earn. I discussed with many people from all over the world about their source of income. During the discussion, one thing was clear. To find the source of income, they were finding the real time challenges at the root level that were faced by people of that village or city or country or the world in the present or future based on statistics and real time data of the past, the present and future predictions. Then they earned money by providing the solutions for that challenge. One common challenge that we all faced was to secure basic survival requirements, such as food, cloth, shelter, security and medication, for ourselves and others. I needed to arrange these things along with some work where money could be earned.

I started visiting my village and neighboring villages to find the sources to earn money, and one thing was clear while visiting villages: I could not do this alone. I needed people who could support me in doing the work. I completely analyzed villages and what they were doing to earn money. I prepared the list for the village to become financially free in order to reconstruct the entire village:
1. Money is a major factor which plays an important role in development. Every transaction into the village should be transparent and available to the public.

2. Money should not be yours or mine, it should be ours. This way everybody is responsible and accountable. We will open one bank in the village and all transactions will happen from there. Nobody keeps money with them; they can withdraw or deposit money from a bank which is trackable, or they should have a proper reason to have money with them, i.e, either they paid or earned it by doing any work.

3. Power should be divided equally among all representatives instead of giving to a single person. One report team, which contains a single representative and his team should be there to monitor everything but they don't have power where they submit reports from starting to ending on every decision and its actions. Every decision that is taken should be finalized based on facts, reality, all representatives' approval and report team.

4. Every single person must respect, help, support, protect and follow all rules and regulations irrespective of their age, religion, gender, occupation, designation, etc.

5. Food, hospital, education, entertainment, homes, clothes are free of cost for everyone and all maintenance will be done by a village bank which maintains money.

6. Everyone is responsible and accountable for every resource they are using: Financial resources, human resources, natural resources, physical resources, political resources, etc.

7. Every single person should be aware, understand the reality of life and death, and be able to detach from both body and mind, then only they are eligible for any responsibility of the village or city or country.

8. People should sacrifice their life and family in extreme situations for the welfare of the village or city or country to solve real-time problems by spending resources, time and effort.

9. Freedom to make their own life choices for themselves or others without hurting others.

10. You can create your own ethical ways to earn money to support the village.

I went to the village head Tribikram to discuss my planning and list to achieve the financial freedom to reconstruct the village.

Tribikram: Tyagaraj, I have gone through your planning and list. I know you are capable of achieving financial freedom to reconstruct our village as per your dream to make "this village the happiest village in this country and world". But before that, I would suggest you discuss your dream, planning, and list with the villagers. This discussion will give you clarity on whether village people will support you or not.

Tyagaraj: Yes, that is more important. Let's discuss this with the villagers this Sunday.

Tribikram: Yes, sure. I will inform everyone. Let's meet all of them on Sunday.
Now it was Saturday night. I couldn't sleep. My old friend Sanani said, "Don't worry, Tyagaraj, everything will be alright. I want you to remember this: accept the decision of the village people, whatever they choose, and work on your dream."

Tyagaraj: Thank you, Sanani for supporting me. I will remember this and work on my dream no matter what the decision is. I am giving my 100%. That's enough for me.

The next day, I woke up and went to a meeting. Everyone was waiting for us. Tribikram gave them the details about my plan and list to **"Detach from body and mind"** and **"Get financial freedom to reconstruct the entire village"**. I discussed my dream with them to make our village **"The happiest village in this country and world"**. After listening to everything, very few people agreed on it but mostly all of them said, "We are happy with what we have and everybody is working based on their needs and desires. The lesser the desires we have, the less we work."

The meeting was over.
I accepted their answer and went to Karnali River to spend some time by myself. When I returned, the conclusion was that they are not ready to change themselves and their village. One thing was clear to me: To implement what I wanted to do, I needed people's support and a village where they would accept the change and were ready for implementation. I questioned myself, **"What is my next plan?"** At that time, it was not clear what I needed to do next. After spending some time at Karnali river, I went home.

Going to the Fair (Mela)

While I was on my way home, a boy was crying. I asked him, "What happened?" He said, "I want to go to the Fair (Mela), but my mom is not taking me." When I talked to his mom, she said, "I have some work and his father has gone for work. No one is there to take him to the mela. You know he does not listen to me when he goes to the Fair. He needs what he sees."
I said, "It reminds me of myself when I was a child. If you don't mind, can I take him to the Fair? At least he will be happy to get what he wants." His mom agreed.
I asked the boy when and where the fair was.
He said, "It is tomorrow in the neighboring village."

That boy and I both went to Fair. We both enjoyed every part of the fair. It was afternoon and we both felt hungry so we both ate at a hotel which is present in a fair. When we started to go through another side of the fair, suddenly the boy started running towards the crowd. When I went there, I found there was an Art Exhibition of different paintings. The boy wanted to go there and see those paintings. I agreed to take him. I purchased 2 coupons for both of us and we waited in the queue.
When we entered the exhibitions, the paintings were very beautiful. There was one painting which caught my attention. When I asked about these paintings, the artist said, "This painting portrays the 100-year calendar of the Human Life Cycle. Every human being lives 100 years maximum on an average. In these 100 years, humans take birth and die at any point of time. If you see these 100 years in front of you then you can plan things in your lives accordingly. Before these 100 years start and after these 100 years are over, you don't exist. Now you exist, so live, enjoy and do whatever you want to do in this life because it's a gift you

receive from nature. There are 2 lives, one, while you exist here and another you live after death. The first one is more important, as you must live your life while you exist here. The other life is if you want to live more than 100 years i.e., after your death. Then you have to do something in life such that you create artifacts of it in the form of something like art, books, documents, videos, audios, gadgets, unique creations, etc. which will be used by all species and human beings. In this way, you will be remembered after you die.

Example: This artist died 10 years back but he is still alive through this painting and he is remembered by everyone who sees this painting."

We both saw the remaining paintings and we left for another exhibition in the fair. We both enjoyed the fair and left for home. I handed the boy to his mom and left for home.

The next day, I went to Karnali river with some papers and a pen. I started to prepare my mind map for the 100 years from birth to death. I listed the things that I had done and the things that I wanted to do in life while I was alive so that people would remember me even after I died.

Document the Dream

One thing was clear to me. During my journey to achieve my dream, I needed to explain about my dream, plan and list to everyone. I can do that but it is a time-consuming process. It is not feasible to explain to everyone about my dream, plan and list. I am not sure how many will understand my objective and perspective about my dream. They understand what they want to understand about it. I will do one thing: I will document everything about my dream, plan and list so that I can ask people to refer to this document to know more about it. I can make copies of it so that people who have similar dreams or goals can use this as a foundation reference to achieve what they want to achieve by modifying this as per their needs. This document can be shared all over the world so that they can achieve things in their lives first and then they change and help their own family, society, village, city, country & world, etc.

I documented my dream to make the village **"The happiest village in this country and world"** by understanding plans and lists to **"Detach from body and mind"** and **"Get financial freedom to reconstruct the entire village"**. I also added some other modules too, such as, how a person can **"Detach from his body and mind"** and **"Get financial freedom in this life"** so that it can be applicable to individuals and society. During my tourism work and this process, I understood while traveling, that I was enjoying my life, and in short, **"Living every moment of my life"**. Most of the time, people forget to live life and achieve everything. I also covered some other things, to live life in every moment so that they can live life and achieve their dream as well. Every moment that they are alive, they should enjoy in every part of life so that from the starting day of their dream till they achieve it and after achieving also, they should live and enjoy every moment of life. Life itself is one big dream and gift.

In life, we have other dreams, so enjoy every moment of life every day.

"Don't wait for occasions in order to be happy; instead of that, make every day an occasion and be happy".

I documented everything and kept it aside. And then I sat on the river side and watch the water flow. I heard a voice from behind calling my name, "Tyagaraj". When I turned around, I saw it was Sanani.

"Hello Sanani, how are you? You came here?"

Sanani: Hello Tyagaraj, I am good. I worried about you after the Village meeting discussion. I thought of meeting you and discussing your next plan.

Tyagaraj: I was disturbed after the village meeting discussion so I came here to understand things from their point of view. I saw they are right from their point of view. While I was going home, I went to the Fair because of a boy. Later, I got lessons from that fair to document my dream to share it with everyone, regardless of my presence. I documented it as a stepping stone to help others.

Could you please check and let me know any updates or corrections are required to make this document more realistic?

Ready with Next Plan

Sanani: Give me one day, I will check and let you know. By the way, what is your next plan? Do you have anything in mind?

Tyagaraj: When I spent some time thinking about my next plan, it was clear to me that this village does not need any modification, they are happy with what they have. I need to find a village where they want to change, modify the village, and live life in a better way by solving their real-time problems. I will go and check all the villages in Jumla, Karnali, and Nepal. If I find any village where people are ready for change as per my dreams then I will spend my life there and apply all my dreams to make that village the happiest village in the country and world. I know this is not easy, but I will give my best to solve every challenge that comes my way to achieve my dream.

Sanani: You have a very good plan. In the worst-case scenario, if you don't find that village in Nepal, what will you do next?

Tyagaraj: I will go and check other countries one by one till I find that village. I also have another alternative plan. I will adopt a village and implement my dream there. I will choose whichever plan is more feasible. Right now, I don't want to decide. During the journey, based on the challenges, I will decide what I need to choose as an option.
Sanani: This is what I can expect from you. Anyway, during your journey if you see, at any point in time, that you require my suggestion or point of view or my help, please don't hesitate to inform me. I am more than happy to help you and be part of your dream.

Tyagaraj: Sure, I will let you know.

Next Day, Sanani came to my place in the morning.

Sanani: I have gone through the documents and I have made some points which need to be modified, and have some questions which I highlighted.

Tyagaraj: Did you eat anything?

Sanani: No, I came here directly.

Tyagaraj: Let's eat something and then we will go to Karnali River to discuss your modifications and questions. Will that be okay?

Sanani: Yes, sure.

Tyagaraj: We both ate and went to Karnali river. We discussed everything. I found some points needed to be added and some modifications were required. So, I updated both of them and said, "This is the next minor version with minor changes. If there are major changes then it's a major version."

Sanani: Why are you taking my points and updating them? This way you will lose your original points, right?

Tyagaraj: This is not my personal dream for myself. In that scenario, I will make my own points and follow them based on my requirements and needs. I don't need other people's point of view there, and even if I get any inputs, I will see and compare with reality to validate whether the point is really genuine or not. If it's genuine then I will definitely accept it and implement it. Here, in this dream, the entire village and many people are involved so the more the contribution I get for my dream, the more the improvement it will go through to make a more unique dream at a global level. I document every version very carefully. I document why I modified it and why I did not modify it so that people can choose whatever version suits them. This way, in my absence, people can make their own version of this dream and they will be connected to this dream through their contribution. I hope it's clear to you, right?

Sanani: Yes, it's clear.

We both discussed and updated the document as per requirements.
Tyagaraj: From tomorrow onwards, I will be in search of a village where I can implement my dream. I will let you know, as soon as I find a village for my dream.

Sanani: Yes, sure.

We both recollected all of our old memories and enjoyed that whole day by doing what makes us happy. We both left for the day.

In Search of a Village

Tyagaraj: I started my search to find a village where I could implement my dream. I went to every village and met the village head. I shared my document with them and explained in detail. Everybody listened and said, "It is a very good idea." But at the end they said, "Sorry, please look for another village."
I accepted their answer and left to see another village. I visited almost 20 villages but nobody was interested.

One day, I was walking in the market and suddenly people started running towards an open garden. I was curious to know why they all suddenly started running. I went behind them and asked, "Why are you all running here?" One person said, "There is a couple here, who provides free food weekly."
I was also feeling hungry, so I also ate with them. While eating, people around me said, "Next week there's a fair (Mela) for a week in our village." Some said yes and some said no. I asked them the location of the fair. They gave me all the details. I just went to that place 3 days prior. When I inquired about it, I found that there were villages nearby and people from almost 10 villages would come to enjoy the fair.

Present My Dream in Fair (Mela)

I got an idea to present my dream to all in the fair by taking a shop, presenting and selling my document along with my contact details. I prepared everything for the fair.

The first day of the fair arrived. I was ready to present my dream. On the first day, nobody came. I knew from the beginning that very few people are interested in my dream. On the next day, 3 people came. I explained my idea to them and shared my document. On the remaining days, 3 to 4 people came every day and I gave my best to explain to them and shared my document so that they could implement whatever they think fit. On the last day, one person asked me a question and his name was **Pritham**.

Pritham: Why are you sharing your dream & documents? This way others can copy your dream and you do not get any credit.

Tyagaraj: I want to change things around me so that people can live their lives to the fullest. During my Tourism work, I went to every country and I found many people died with their dream which they once wanted to fulfill. In any case, if they had documented and shared it with others then at least their dream would have lived and it would reach those people who make themself capable enough to achieve it by going through challenges and difficulties. This way at least that person would have lived on after his death.

Types of Dreams

There is something, I want to clear about my dream. When I researched and meditated on the word 'dream', I found, there are 2 types of dreams that people work to achieve. One kind of dream is for oneself and the other kind of dream is for the public.

The Self kind of dream is where people want to keep it private. They want credit, recognition, name, fame, money, etc. from it. They don't want to share it with anyone, including their family and friends. They die with its secrets irrespective of whether they achieved it or not.
Another Self kind of dream is where people want to share it with only limited people like their family or friends or colleagues. They also want credit, recognition, name, fame, money, etc. from it. They die happily for, at least they lived their dream and shared it with the limited people to make their dream live on after they died.

The Public kind of dream is where that person wants to share it with everyone so that people can live and experience it. This way, their dream and they will live forever on this earth even after their death. This dream is not for them, it's for humanity. Here they don't want any credit, recognition, name, fame, money, etc. All they want is their dream to be useful to humanity in one or the other way. This way they are happy from within, that at least they have made a difference in people's lives and give meaning to their life.
I also wish for the same thing and want to make my dream publicly available so that people all over the world can implement my dream in their villages to change their life and experience a new way of life.

Pritham: You are a very noble man. Can you give me one example so that I can understand it?

Tyagaraj: Yes, sure. Let me give you my example of why I decided to choose this path.

Understanding A Different Perspective

During Tourism work, when I got an opportunity to work on the "Survey on Happiest and Saddest Countries in the World", I was going to all the countries for a survey. We went to Russia. I was asking basic survey questions to a lady. Her name was Elizabeth. She asked, "To which lady are you asking?"

I said, "As I can see, you are the only woman standing here, so it's clear I am asking you."

Elizabeth laughed and said, "I know you are asking me. Let me give you a clarification so that you can understand. Within me there are 2 ladies. One who thinks and detaches herself from this body and mind, and calls herself 'Life'. She is able to see this whole world from that perspective by thinking of everyone as Life. The other lady is the one who thinks of herself as this body and mind. She is able to see this whole world from that perspective by thinking of everyone as body and mind. It is the default understanding of every single person from birth that they are this body and mind. People live all their life in this body and mind so they think and experience this body and mind as they want to. But when people try to live life and death consciously then they start experiencing that they are not this body and mind, by living every moment consciously. Once they realize that their journey of life is totally going in a different direction, then they see life totally from a different perspective as per reality.
Let me give you an example so that you can understand it. This is a lighter. Right now, I am aware and experienced that I am not this body and mind. I am burning my left-hand's little finger for 1 minute and then I'm applying honey on it. This is happening consciously, that's why I am able to observe it silently as though I

am an Observer. Sometimes my body gets hurt during any incident. At that time also I am able to observe it silently like an Observer."

Tyagaraj: I am really shocked that you lit the lighter, burned your little finger for a minute and applied honey after a minute. You were completely silent, as though it was happening to another person altogether. I also saw that you hardly blinked your eye. How can you detach from your body and mind? Does it happen every time you wish to do it? How does it work? What is the perspective you are talking about?

Elizabeth: First you need to be aware that you are not this body and mind. Whatever happens to your body, just keep silent, close your mouth and watch. Once you experience the silence, and observe what is happening to your body and where it hurts physically. Then you get separated from this body such that you only observe like an observer. Once you experience detachment from the body then it will be there forever. From that day onwards, you just observe everything happening to your body and you will take care of this body's health because you exist here because of this body. The mind takes all the inputs through our sense organs and stores it in our memory through images and voices. The 5 Sense Organs are: eyes (for seeing), nose (for smelling), ears (for hearing), tongue (for tasting), and skin (for touching or feeling). Our sense organs always watch outside our body, that's why we think the solutions to our problems are outside. We seek solutions outside where we always get into new problems because we are not understanding that the root cause of a problem and its solution are inside. Once we are able to focus our sense organs within ourselves, we will see that all our needs, desires, dreams and goals are built for this body through mind. By taking our sense organs inward at one point in time we will observe and conquer our mind. Then we will start observing our mind, emotions, feelings and everything that is happening to this body and mind. Once you see the reality of life i.e., death (body will be taken by nature), then you start living the life where you built the desires, dreams and goals based on life. Here you and life are not separate, **you are that life which is experiencing this existence through this body and mind on this earth with the help of nature.** This way you will be able to connect with everyone in life by looking into their eyes. You will do things beyond imagination, and people will get peace within when they are near and connected to you without their knowledge. Once their understanding about life is questioned by themselves by taking their sense organs inward then they start and experience life within them.

As per your survey, happiest and saddest countries happen because people live by understanding themselves as the body and mind. Once they are able to detach from this body and experience this life, they would start experiencing this life and they'd work on themselves first because those people's **actions speak louder than their words.** They take care of themselves first, their family, their friends and society. They are unable to keep anything with them, so they start sharing everything they have, from money to knowledge and experience. But very few people recognize and understand their wisdom. This way they are able to see everyone all over the world with love, compassion, kindness and forgiveness by filling their life with happiness.

I hope you understand the question, "To which lady are you asking?"

Tyagaraj: Yes, I understood the question now and the right answer to it as well. Thank you so much for opening my eyes.

I left for another country to complete my survey. Once the survey was completed, I went to a nearby garden and thought about it. Then I started to experience detachment from body and mind. My whole understanding and experience of life turned upside down. From there my journey changed from tourism to my village because of my dream. Then I started to make this document. I hope you understand my example.

Pritham: Yes, I understood very well. Thank you.

That was the last day of the fair. I also left for another village to find the right village. Again, I visited 10 villages in the next couple of months.

At Last, I Found the Village Where I Could Implement My Dream

One day, I went to a village. I met the village head and I opened my document to explain about my dream, then the village head said, "I have seen this document before. Let me recollect it. Yes, I remember this document. Are you Tyagaraj?"
I said, "Yes. I am Tyagaraj."
The village head told that his name is Deepak.

Deepak: My son bought this document. He reviewed your document and he already implemented some of these things in our village. I asked my son to bring you to implement these things in our village but he said that you will definitely come here one day. Till that time he asked me to let him prepare our village, so that whenever you visit, we can show you that we are working on your dream.

By listening to all these things, suddenly I had tears in my eyes.

Tyagaraj: I am very happy, that at last I found the village where I can implement my dream.

I observed Pritham coming home and he was shocked to see me at his home.

Pritham: Finally, you are here, as I expected.
Tyagaraj: How did you know that I will come here?
Pritham: It's simple, when we truly dedicate and prepare ourselves for something then definitely that kind of people will surely meet each other one day.

I understood his words completely. We both hugged each other. He greeted me well and we both ate together. The next day, I wrote a letter to my friend Sanani that I found the village where I could implement my dream.

Pritham and I started discussing many things about our source of income, to get financial freedom to implement many things in our village. We created many exercises to experience detachment from body and mind.

These are the things we followed to achieve, "Get Financial Freedom to reconstruct the entire village" & "Detach from Body and Mind to Experience new Life".

Get Financial Freedom to Reconstruct the Entire Village

1. We opened one bank in the village where all transactions happen. Nobody would keep money with them; they could withdraw or deposit money from a bank which is trackable, or they must have a proper reason to have money, i.e, either they have paid or earned by doing any work. Every transaction in the village should be transparent and available to the public. Everybody is responsible and accountable. Money should not be yours or mine, it should be ours.

2. The entire village started joint farming and the amount was directly deposited to the bank.

3. Fish Farming started as Karnali river passed nearby villages.

4. Attracting tourists by modifying and creating some unique things in the village. Example: unique cooking tastes, paintings, adventure gardens, rebuilding of cultural monuments, etc.

5. We started building unique homes with least facilities to all the facilities in order that people need to change their homes on monthly basis so that they can detach from both homes and clothes.

6. Food, hospitals, education, entertainment, homes, and clothes are free of cost for everyone and all maintenance will be taken care of by village bank.

7. Identifying and solving the real time challenges at the root level that are faced by people of this village.

8. People sacrifice their life and family in extreme situations for the welfare of a village or city or country to solve real time problems by spending resources, giving time and effort.

9. People can create their own ethical ways to earn money to support the village.

Detach From Body and Mind to Experience New Life

1. Understand and observe the life process: birth, life & death. Once they experience life by detaching from body and mind then they flow with basic nature. Awareness of mind and body: (This helps me to understand and experience the separation between mind and me because I am aware of my body parts working during activities).

2. Everybody in this village can be happy and smile when they interact with anyone. Respect everyone, like villagers, visitors, and tourists.

3. In every corner of the village, crematorium grounds are there, inside that place there are very unique games. Everyone comes and plays those games irrespective of their age.

4. Every natural resource available in this village is very protected, like trees, plants, rivers, animals, birds, pets, soil, sand, land, stones, food materials, etc.

5. People should be able to see and observe their body silently by keeping their mouth close whenever it hurts physically, knowingly or unknowingly.

6. Working with eyes and breath to live the present moment.

7. Statue Position: My eyes were open without blinking and my legs were completely touching the ground and not moving at all in standing position. It was as though my legs were attached

to the ground. During this process, I experienced that my bottom is connected to the top.

10. Try to listen to the heart beat by standing or sitting in one place. i.e., in statue position. (It takes time; try to listen to the heartbeat and if you are able to listen then try to do it for 30 minutes.)

11. Give a pause for 5 seconds in between any daily activity that you do, like reading, walking, talking, eating, or anything that is possible to pause for a few seconds.

12. I started walking inside the deep-water carrying weight on my hands till my breath supported it.

13. Be aware and conscious of the energy that is flowing through the five sense organs through this body and mind. Example: Open your eyes and maintain eye contact while talking and close your eyes when you are alone. Talk only if required otherwise keep quiet. Hear outside when you are in public otherwise hear the heartbeat inside. In simple words "Learn to use your energy awarely and consciously so that you can learn to shift your energy wherever required either inside or outside."

14. You can create your own exercise. (The aim of this exercise is to detach from both body and mind).

This way, I & Pritham started working on our dream.

Tyagaraj's Marriage

After 6 months, while I was working, I received information from a person that a foreigner was asking for me. I said, "I am coming, let me complete this work." After completing that work, I went to the visitor's house where I was shocked to see Elizabeth. I asked, "How are you? What are you doing here?"

Elizabeth: I am good. I got your document through my colleague then I thought of meeting you so I came here to see you and your dream.

We both talked for a while. I told her everything about my dream and how I found this village. We both ate together. We both left for the day. Next day, I went to the visitor's room.
Tyagaraj: Hello Elizabeth. What are your plans for today?

Elizabeth: Seeing the village.

Tyagaraj: If you are okay, can I take you through this village?

Elizabeth: Yes sure.

Tyagaraj: We both visited the village. 1 month passed. One day while I was working, I heard Elizabeth's voice.

Elizabeth: What are you doing here?

I said, "I am going through some challenges currently."
Elizabeth: Okay, I want to talk to you in person. Please let me know when you are free.

Tyagaraj: You wait in the garden; I am coming in just 10 minutes.

Elizabeth: Okay sure.

I finished my work and went to the garden.

Tyagaraj: Hi Elizabeth, yes, tell me.

Elizabeth: I wanted to ask you something.

Tyagaraj: Yes, tell me.

Elizabeth: I am looking for someone who understands life and I found you. I want to marry you, Tyagaraj, because you experienced the life which I told you long back.

Tyagaraj: I was about to ask you next week about marriage but luckily you asked first. I accept it. I am also looking for someone who understands life but has not found it so far.

We both married in everyone's presence. We both lived happily by understanding each other. Both of us were working on our village dream.

After working with everyone in this village, everything happened as per our plans. It took 4 years to make our dream come through. People started to visit our village and enjoy everything in the village. This way our village got popular. Many locals and foreigners started taking documents from here and updating as per their requirements after they lived here for 1 month. In the last 4 years, I had 2 kids: one boy and one girl.

Message From the King

One day, we got a message from the King.

Me and Pritham both visited the King's palace. We saw all the important people present over there, the king, the president, the prime minister, and the government officials.

King: I received all the information about what you are doing in that village and this way, people in your village go against our rules.

Tyagaraj: We are not going against your rules, my king. We are following all the rules but there are no problems in our village and we all manage our financial wealth, so we are totally independent monetarily. I request my dear king to provide approval to fulfill our dream in this village.

King: What can you do to save your dream, Tyagaraj?

Tyagaraj: Anything my dear King.

King: Think before saying anything in front of me.

Tyagaraj: I mean, what do I say, my king?

King: I heard about burning the little finger of the left hand. Is it true?

Tyagaraj: Yes, my king. It's true.

King: I will give you one promise. No one will touch your village for a lifetime and your village people can do what they want to do in that village, but on only one condition.

Tyagaraj: Thank you my king, but what is the condition?

King: It's very simple. What you did at a small level, I want you to do it on a big level.

Tyagaraj: I didn't get you, my king. Can you please elaborate?

King: Yes sure, why not. In front of everyone we will burn you and you have to keep silent and become an Observer. If you remain silent until you burn completely then we will free your village and no one will touch your village for life.

Tyagaraj: I am ready, my king. Let me know when it is planned. I am happy to witness such an event to prove to a larger audience that detachment from body and mind can be possible to experience Life.

King: Are you serious, Tyagaraj? You will die.

Tyagaraj: Yes, my king, I am serious. As per my experience of life, my body and mind will unite with nature. I will witness myself. In other words, people call it death. There is a difference in understanding and experiencing life, which gives different definitions of the same word. That's it, my king.

King: I am giving you one month to complete all your work and spend time with your family. Next month, on the same date I will come to your village for your death.

Tyagaraj: Thank you, king, for giving me some time to complete some pending works.

I and Pritham both went home. We called everyone in the village for meeting and told them everything that happened in the king's palace. Everybody was silent. I said, "The day I started to search for a village, I was ready to witness myself without this body and mind. I am very lucky that at least I have fulfilled my dream and this dream will live on, even after I die as well because of the liveness of the dream which I documented. People from all over the world will come here to experience life without this body and mind whenever they are ready. I am happy to get all this time to spend with you."

My wife was also there in the crowd. When I saw her eyes, she was smiling. When I went home, I said, "I am happy that at least you understand me and smiled at me in the meeting."

Elizabeth: I know you from the beginning. In these 4 years, we both experienced a kind of life that nobody ever experienced. I know our body is just an instrument; we were separated from this body the day we experienced the separation from body and mind. That's why I smiled.

Tyagaraj: As we both prepared the document for our children when they mature in life, they will get the options to choose which life they want based on their desires and actions. If they want to experience this life then this village will be a living example to them. If they don't want to, then it's their own choice. Whatever the choice they are taking, as a parent I respect them.

I talked with Pritham and said, "I don't have anything to tell you. You and the village people run this village based on your understanding and requirements. It's not only my dream, it's our dream so I am happy at least my foundation helped to build this village. If I was not there at the beginning then definitely someone could have done the foundation. Do you have anything for me, Pritham?"

Pritham: No, Tyagaraj. I'm very happy to have you in my village.

The day had come. The King and all the other officials came to our village. Tyagaraj was taken into the garden; he sat quietly at the center. King arranged oil cups and requested everyone to pour the oil onto Tyagaraj's body. Everybody, including his wife and children, completed putting the oil on his body. He was smiling at everyone. The King asked for any last wish from Tyagaraj. Tyagaraj just smiled and said nothing. Then the king set fire to Tyagaraj. As the king requested, Tyagaraj kept silent and became an Observer. It took 1 hour to completely burn Tyagaraj but nobody listened to anything from him. During the burning also, he was smiling. As promised, he was silent all the time and became an Observer.

At the end, King said, "As I promised to Tyagaraj, no one will touch this village for a lifetime and the village people can do whatever they want to do. I want you to make a statue of Tyagaraj with his ashes.
I did this intentionally to prove everyone in this world that conscious and aware people about life are always ready to sacrifice everything, including their life for humanity to welfare of people and society."

Gyanraj: This is all about the story of Tyagaraj and this village which changed everything in this village. Like I said, this entire village has wise people because they experienced life.

Reach Those People Who Seek the Truth Of Life

I hope you got your answers, Naveen.

Naveen: Yes, I got all the answers. We both spent 2 months in that village and went back home to Mumbai.

I thanked Gyanraj for showing his village and sharing this beautiful story to help me understand life. While I was going home, Gyanraj gifted me with a small token of love.

When I opened it, I was surprised to see that it was a document copy of Tyagaraj's dream. I hugged Gyanraj and thanked him very much. We both left for the day.

I started to go through the document and I prepared my own notes and paintings. I implemented everything that was there in the document, in my life and I also documented everything that I experienced all these years, and life changing stories from different perspectives in those notes and paintings. I prepared all these notes and paintings because one day they would reach those people who seek the truth of life. Thank you everyone.

Dinesh: Vinod, these are all the stories of Naveen which I have kept with me for so many days without sharing them with anyone because I didn't find anyone who seeks the truth of life. But when I met you and saw your actions, I was unable to stop myself from sharing all these things with you.

I have created my dream of an **"Autonomous Village"** by referring to Tyagaraj's dream document and I created my own version based on some updates and modifications as per my dream. I have implemented and experienced the "Detach from body and mind" points and I modified something in them based on experience.

Now if you go through our conversion from when we met for the first time till date then you will understand each and every point which I said to you in a totally different perspective from the first one. It's your choice to recollect our conversation from the start to understand life in a better way, once again.

Now you decide whether we need to involve these stories in our dream or not.

Vinod: I will suggest that you include these stories in our Library. Whoever seeks the truth of life they will definitely reach these stories one way or the other.

We will continue to work with our dream of an **Autonomous Village** i.e., the **"Village of Dreams"** so that it can help all those people who truly want to change their life by putting in effort and giving time with patience and consistency.

This is all about the dream which we had and it changed everyone's life including me by making us understand the truth about life.

You can contact the Publisher at:
www.fanatixxpublication.com

www.ingramcontent.com/pod-product-compliance
Lightning Source LLC
LaVergne TN
LVHW061607070526
838199LV00078B/7202